Praise for *All the Rules Have Changed*

"Matt's message of taking control of your finances is more important than ever and his book shows you how. No one can predict the future, but if you follow Matt's advice you can be assured that you'll have one."

Dr. Jack Marrion
Advantage Compendium

"Matt Rettick never fails to deliver! I have known him for many years as both a friend and business associate. Matt, and my husband Jack, co-authored their previous book, Fiscal Fitness and together we forged a lasting partnership. Matt's honesty and integrity shine as he guides the reader through his early personal financial woes and ultimate path to success. He leaves no stone unturned and lays out a bright future for all who follow his plan. "

Elaine LaLanne
Wife to the late, great Jack LaLanne

"I couldn't put this book down. In a financial world that's been derailed by excess noise, hype, and spin, Matt puts consumers and advisors back on track to achieving their financial freedom. He has written a true insider's look at how to win in the game of life, both personally and financially. Read this book as if your finances – and your life – depend on it!"

Steve McCarty, Chairman
National Ethics Association
www.ethicscheck.com

"I know about the sleepless nights suffered by many Americans because they are worried about uncertainty in retirement. Luckily, that doesn't have to be you: Matt Rettick has a plan to put your finances back on track so you can sleep peacefully knowing your financial future is well planned."

Ron Grensteiner
President, American Equity Life Insurance

"Matthew Rettick found inspiration from a biblical passage that turned his financial life around. Readers of his book will be inspired to build a purposeful financial plan to help them achieve goals that are in line with their values."

Barbara Whelehan
Assistant Managing Editor at Bankrate.com

"Matt Retticks's story grabs you by the throat and doesn't let go. His is the tale of the American Dream gone wrong—and then finally, gloriously right. His wisdom is born from the hard experiences that many Americans share. It's a story of redemption and a message filled with insight and advice that you need to hear NOW!"

Frank Maselli
Founder of The Financial Lifeguard Academy

"Matt Rettick is a role model—he lives what he preaches. Matt's real intent is to expose the truth about finance and investing, even if it's the hard truth. It's not always easy to say what the reality is. So many of the talking heads out there try to give assurance where there isn't any. Instead, Matt points out the harsh reality of the situation and says, 'now that we've exposed it, let's figure out how to deal with it.' That's what separates him from other people in the industry."

R. Travis Terlau, CFP®
Founder and CEO of Louisville, Ky.-based Investment Answers™
www.InvestmentAnswers.net

"As Matt shares in this book, the New Financial Reality has arrived. Now, more than ever, it's important to work hard to protect investments, pay off debt, minimize fees and create a financial strategy that works for you and your specific situation."

Chris Cook
President, Beacon Capital Management
www.BeaconInvesting.com

"As a longtime member of the Financial Planning Association, Matthew Rettick knows firsthand of the importance of retirement planning for all Americans. Rettick's book will help consumers understand how the playing field has changed and how important it is to adjust their outlook to create a financial plan that will last a lifetime."

Lauren M. Schadle, CAE
CEO, Financial Planning Association

"Matthew takes the complexities of today's economy and the myriad decisions facing current and future retirees and provides straight-forward and balanced information. In a financial world that's been derailed by excess noise, hype, and spin, Matt gives you a true insider's look at how to win."

Kim O'Brien
President & CEO, NAFA
www.nafa.com
NAFA, the National Association for Fixed Annuities, is a national trade association exclusively dedicated to promoting the awareness and understanding of fixed annuities.

"Yes, the rules have been changed – by investment firms, giant banks, lenders, insurers and dysfunctional government at all levels. What can the responsible citizen do? Read Matt's book in order to understand the risks, evaluate the options, make wise financial decisions--and take action starting now!"

Ed Morrow, CLU, ChFC, RFC
International Association of Registered Financial Consultants

"All the Rules Have Changed" by Matthew Rettick reminds us that the road to lifetime financial security is often obstructed by taxes, debt, health issues, Wall Street corruption, the unexpected and sometimes paralysis from not knowing what to do or who to trust. But all of these roadblocks are removable because they can be planned for - and you'll find a workable and sensible game plan right here."

Ed Slott, CPA
Founder of www.irahelp.com

ALL THE RULES HAVE CHANGED

WHAT YOU MUST DO TO SUCCEED IN THE NEW FINANCIAL REALITY

MATT RETTICK
Creator of *The Checks and Balances Financial Success System™*

Published by CBTV Publishing, Nashville, Tennessee.

The following are registered trademarks of Checks and Balances TV:
Checks and Balances TV
America's #1 Source for Balanced Financial Advice
Checks and Balances Financial Success System
The New Financial Reality

Permissions Department
CBTV Publishing
22 Century Boulevard, Suite 450
Nashville, TN 37214
info@ChecksandBalances.TV

Printed in the United States of America

CBTV books are available at special quantity discounts. For more information, please contact the publisher at (615) 620-1860 or info@ChecksandBalances.TV. www.ChecksandBalances.TV
ISBN: 978-0-9885571-0-9

Dedication

To my wonderful children—Greg, Candy, Jeremy, and Brandon, and my 13 grandchildren and great grandson, Aric. I have been blessed beyond measure by having each of you in my life. Your love, energy, faith, and forgiveness have inspired me to press on and become a better man, father, and grandfather.

My hopes are that this book will help you (and everyone else who reads it) better prepare for today's New Financial Reality.

Acknowledgments

- To Mark Patterson, a special thanks for your vision of CBTV, as well as your gifted talents in designing the cover of this book. You are a true friend and a genius in helping people find their unique brand.

- To Alana Kohl, thanks so very much for being my ace researcher and writer for CBTV, as well as a very close friend.

- To Susan Marks, an amazing journalist and writer, and co-collaborator in creating this book.

- To Cynthia Zigmund, thank you for your direction and guidance in reviewing and making suggestions to each draft manuscript, as well as helping me with every step in the book-creation process. You are a terrific resource and friend!

- To Melissa Longbrake, my long-suffering personal assistant. You never cease to amaze me how you come through for me, no matter the time of the day or night or weekend that I call upon you. You are truly God-sent to me.

- To my son, Jeremy Rettick, thank you for your research and advice, as well as your belief that your dad can do almost anything.

- To Jessica Duke, a gifted young woman who helps me on a daily basis with her creative graphic designs and PowerPoint presentations.

- To Pete Winer, man I miss you so very much Pete! God took you way too soon. Thanks for your incredible passion for writing about how financial products really work and the financial-services industry. You were a true financial insider.

- To Joe Stamps, thanks for your commitment to the life insurance industry and to me in helping educate Americans about the "living" benefit of life insurance, as well as the death benefits.

- To some amazing supportive women in my life—my daughter, Candy Rettick; my daughter-in-laws, Nomi Rettich and Carla Martinez; my sister Cathy MacPherson; my sister-in-law Michele Rettich; my good friend and founder of Mercy Ministries, Nancy Alcorn; my wonderful family counselor and friend, Margaret Phillips; the co-leader of the Divorce Care Class and support group in Nashville, Tennessee, Margaret Wilson, and two wonderful women of God who are so well-grounded in their faith and their marriage, Kelly Terlau and Betty Jones. Without all of you, this book would never have been published. Thank you!

- To my wonderful clients who agreed to be interviewed for this book: Norma Spear, Dr. Jack and Anne Riley Miller, Matthew Kennedy, the unconquerable Helen Bratcher, and Ms. Eunice Sears.

- To my terrific personal administrative assistant for ten years, Barbara Hansen.

- To the "True Financial Advisors" with whom I have the pleasure of working and who volunteered their time to be interviewed for this book, Ron Roberts, David Wilcox, Travis Terlau, John Evans, John Eikenberry, and Jim Jones. And, to my business associate and friend J.R. Thacker, thank you for allowing me to use excerpts from your book, *Index Interest: The Missing Asset Class* (Resource Media LLC).

- And to my good personal friend and early mentor, TC.

- To the wonderful people at Bookmasters, thank you!

- To my Lord and Savior Jesus Christ, thank you for giving me life and the passion to make a difference in the lives of other people.

- And to you the reader, I have been where you are today. I know first-hand the pain of a life of financial failure. The good news is that I also know how to crawl out of that pit and onto solid financial ground. So, let's walk together so that one day you will be financially free!

Foreword

As I write this at the start of 2013, I'm experiencing very mixed emotions. From a national perspective, I'm happy that the Congress and the President reached a deal to avoid the "fiscal cliff," because the alternative would have likely plunged the country back into recession and increased our nation's employment and under-employment challenges. The bad news is the deal did not meaningfully address the drivers of our nation's structural deficits and mounting debt, and they have set the country up for another debt ceiling fight that could be damaging to the fragile economic recovery.

We should not be surprised. During the past 10 years or so, millions of Americans, including me and members of my family, have grown disgusted with the current state of political affairs in Washington. Contrary to the desires of our nation's founders, our federal political system is dominated by career politicians, many of whom lack the practical real-world experience and perspective to do their jobs effectively. This fact, combined with the current hyper-partisanship, great ideological divide, and the undue influence of a broad-range of special interest groups, have created stalemate in Washington in connection with a range of large and growing challenges facing our nation.

Sadly, unlike at the outset of our Republic, we now have too many laggards rather than leaders in Washington, D.C. Elected officials are more concerned with keeping their jobs and satisfying the political and ideological base of their own party rather than doing their jobs and working for the broader public interest and the greater good. Too many are focused on today and not taking steps to create a better tomorrow. For the future of our country and families, this must change and soon.

On a more personal and positive note, I recently became debt free for the second time in my adult life on December 21. My wife, Mary, and I don't believe in the Mayan and Hopi calendars and were confident that the sun would rise on December 22—it did. Selling our former primary residence in Mt. Vernon, Virginia, enabled us to pay off the mortgage on our current primary residence in the Black Rock section of Bridgeport, Connecticut.

We were able to pay off all our debt and be well positioned for retirement in large part because we planned, budgeted, saved, invested, and preserved most of our savings during our lifetimes. Throughout the years, we also budgeted for things that many people don't, namely savings for a home, cars, our children's education, and our own retirement as well as charitable contributions. In our view, you need to plan for your and your family's future, and help others less well off at the same time.

While I and many other American recognize the importance of planning and saving, the U.S. government evidently does not. Believe it or not, despite being in business for almost 225 years as a Republic, the U.S. government still does not have a strategic planning framework. In addition, it has only passed timely annual budgets and spending bills four times in my 61-year lifespan. It also doesn't have a portfolio of outcome-based performance statistics to determine whether its many spending programs, tax policies, and regulatory practices are working. And we wonder why government has financial, performance, and accountability problems.

What do these items have to do with this book on personal finance? Quite a lot. From a national perspective, I hope that our elected leaders finally come together and achieve a fiscal "Grand Bargain" in 2013. Such a Grand Bargain should include a range of budget controls, social insurance reforms, comprehensive tax reform, and defense and other spending reductions designed to address the large and growing structural deficits and mounting debt burdens that lie ahead. If left unaddressed, they will lead us to the edge of what I have referred to as a fiscal abyss. We must change course in order not to fall into this abyss. It represents our real fiscal challenge, while the fiscal cliff was just a symptom of an addiction to deficits and debt.

Despite assertions to the contrary, both political parties have allowed the federal government to grow too big and promise too much over the years. In recent years, Washington has been operating in accordance with Democratic spending policies and Republican taxing practices. The combination of big spending and low taxes, coupled with weak economic growth, international conflicts, and domestic events, have led to large deficits and mounting debt burdens. These will get worse over time absent a change in course due to the retirement of the Baby Boom generation, rising health care costs, and an outdated tax system.

Basic financial prudence says that you can't spend a lot more than you take in and not expect to have a day of reckoning at some point. Therefore, the time has come to restructure the federal government.

It's not a matter of whether the needed federal restructuring will happen, it's only a matter of when and how. Hopefully, our elected officials will act prudently, pre-emptively, and before a U.S. debt crisis is at our doorstep. Otherwise, the United States could have to adopt sudden and draconian spending cuts and tax increases like Greece. This does not have to happen, and our elected officials should make sure that it doesn't happen.

Irrespective of when our elected officials act, it is clear that the federal government will have to significantly reduce projected spending in the future and raise taxes above historical levels. That means the federal government will do less and tax more in future years. Yes, you read that correctly.

Given this outlook, states and localities will not receive as much assistance from the federal government, and they should start now to adjust their promises and change their practices accordingly. In addition, charities will become even more important as part of our nation's social safety net.

From an individual perspective, the inevitable restructuring of the federal government will mean that tens of millions of individual Americans will have to assume a greater responsibility for their own financial future. All things considered, the younger a person is and the more income and wealth a person has, the more he or she will be impacted by the coming changes in government spending programs and tax policies. That is appropriate because the younger one is, and the more resources one has, the more time and ability one has to make needed adjustments.

And what about debt? Not all debt is equal. Some level of debt is acceptable, and even advisable, under some circumstances. However, too much debt is not. After all, interest is the cost of taking on debt, and you don't get anything for interest.

Both from a government and personal perspective, some debt can be investment-related (e.g., critical infrastructure, basic research, education, primary residence) and some can be consumption-related (e.g., recurring and/or non-essential expenses). Some debt may be required due to extraordinary events (e.g., wars, major disasters, serious personal accidents, or illnesses).

Therefore, it's important to understand not just how much debt you have, but also what the debt you have relates to. Debt should not be used to finance recurring expenses or unneeded and imprudent individual wants.

Individuals should not follow the bad example of the federal government, and this book, *All the Rules Have Changed*, provides comprehensive, clear, and compelling ideas that will help individuals help themselves to create a better financial future. It is written in a user-friendly fashion and includes a number of personal anecdotes by the author, Matt Rettick, to help bring key messages alive.

I am certain that you will find the information and advice in this book to be helpful, and I hope that you will put it to good use. I believe strongly in the concept of leading by example. I have tried to do so throughout my adult life. Reading this book and heeding its advice can help you do so, too.

Hon. David M. Walker
Former U.S. Comptroller General
Bridgeport, Connecticut

Contents

Part III:
You Can Do It!

Now you can have a system to help you make critical financial decisions and you'll never have to say, "If I only knew then…" because, *Now You Know!*

— MATT RETTICK

The Five Financial Truths™
In the New Financial Reality

FINANCIAL TRUTH 1: The Financial World Is Biased.

You can't believe everything you read or hear as absolute truth. Everyone is trying to sell you something to make a buck. Stop believing that anyone really cares as much about *your* financial success as you do.

FINANCIAL TRUTH 2: It's Not That Complicated.

The financial world is really not as complicated as the so-called experts want you to believe. You don't have to have an MBA degree from Harvard Business School of Finance to make good financial decisions regarding your life and your future.

FINANCIAL TRUTH 3: Consider the Pros and Cons.

Every (legal) investment product or savings vehicle has its pros and cons, pluses and minuses, advantages and disadvantages. It's up to you to consider and understand both sides of the coin. Don't take anyone's advice who says, "Never buy that investment." Why not listen to them? Because they're showing their bias.

FINANCIAL TRUTH 4: It's Your Responsibility.

You have a responsibility to investigate the facts yourself and make a Checks and Balances financial decision with every purchase or investment you make. Your financial future depends on your willingness and ability to do your own research and investigation.

FINANCIAL TRUTH 5: You Must Have a Guide.

You must have a trusted guide to help you on your journey to financial freedom. You can't go it alone anymore; there is simply too much to learn and know on your own. You need to find and work with a "true financial advisor," someone who is more interested in helping you achieve your dreams than in how much money he or she can make on your investments!

"Dump debt, invest wisely, believe in yourself, and make it happen."

— MATT RETTICK

Introduction

My goal is to help you understand the New Financial Reality we live in today and how it impacts you and your money. I want to share with you how you can embrace the true and proven way to get control of your finances and your life—one small step at a time, and once and for all. No matter your circumstances, with the right guidance you can do it.

Too many money "experts" and advice-givers in their cushy corner offices claim to understand what it takes for you and me to get ahead financially. They claim to empathize and know what you're going through. In reality, though, most of them don't really get it—the personal struggles, the disappointments, the stress, or how to really end the cycle of debt and financial despair.

I do. I've lived through the financial struggles, stress, and hardships. I've tried the get-rich-quick schemes and I've failed miserably—multiple times. I've been a single parent trying to pay the rent, the babysitter, and child support, and still put food on the table. I've been unemployed many times and desperately took any job to pay the bills. I've lost my car, fretted how to keep the house warm, been crippled by credit-card debt, and faced foreclosure—not just once, but twice. I've stood by helplessly and watched my grandparents lose everything—including their dignity. I've gambled everything and failed.

I also finally learned the way to get ahead. One day in church with my wife, I was listening to a passage from the Bible (Malachi 3:10) when I had an epiphany. The words that were recited that morning were meant for me. It was my awakening. My spirit literally jumped out of my skin when I heard the words of that passage, and I knew I had to accept the challenge that lay before me. In that moment, I realized that life is about much more than material objects and instant gratification. At last I understood that I had allowed "stuff"—and the cost of that stuff—to take control of my life. I got mad—at myself, at my debt, and at what I had allowed the system to do to me—and I decided to dig my way out. I did it one small step at a time. It wasn't easy, but it certainly was worth it. With the right information and the help of a trusted financial advisor, you, too, can gain control of your money and face the New Financial Reality head on. I promise.

I've spent the last two decades in the financial services industry, and I get that, too—all of it. I understand how financial products and services are marketed and sold. I know the ins and outs, the truth and the lies, and I am here to help you get past the hype and make the right moves. No matter what anyone tells you, not all products are appropriate for every consumer. Every financial product has its pros and cons, advantages and disadvantages that consumers need to know before they buy. Investing is never risk free. Too many people, unfortunately, have found that out the hard way.

I also understand the real motivation of some financial professionals out there. I'm fed up with the self-serving hype that inundates many of us under the guise of "good financial advice." Everyone deserves a fighting chance to regain his or her financial freedom. That's why I wrote this book and launched Checks and Balances TV (online at www.ChecksandBalances.TV).

Forget the promises of get-rich-quick schemes and the need for greed. Don't fall prey to "keeping up with the Joneses," either. They're probably broke, too!

Instead, prepare to face today's New (and different) Financial Reality and make the financial moves that are right for you, your situation, and your responsibilities. Successfully handling your finances is not complicated, and each of us can do it with the right commitment to get ahead.

Introduction

Your journey begins with facing up to the facts. The economic landscape is different today, and the changes are here to stay:

- You're probably not going to get rich beyond your wildest dreams. But that's OK. You still can achieve all that's important to you.

- Don't expect to make lots of money off the stock market. The Dow Jones Industrial Average may (or may not) have averaged gains of more than 10 percent a year since 1928, but who has the 80-plus years to see if it makes them wealthy?

- The government isn't going to take care of you, now or later. Government entitlement programs—including Medicaid, Medicare, and Social Security—are in trouble.

- Job security—and the benefits that came with it, including a lifetime pension when you retire—is gone forever. You're on your own. Small businesses, entrepreneurship, and lean corporate machines power today's economy.

- Your home's equity will never again be a reliable source for pulling out an equity line of credit or a supplement to your income in retirement. Just look at what the recent recession did to home equity in 2008 and 2009.

- Health-care costs are rising so rapidly that unless you're prepared, they'll destroy you and those you love.

- Retirement has been retired! Age 80 has become the new 65. Many of those who reach 65 and want to quit their job can't because of economics. Many people really don't want to retire; they just want more control over what they do.

These are the facts of this New Financial Reality, a reality that requires each of us to take a new approach to money not only to make ends meet, but ultimately to thrive in the financial aspect of our lives and achieve our personal dreams—whatever they are.

As an insider in the world of finance, I am here to guide you on your way to your true and lasting financial freedom. In the pages of this book, and with the help of my website, www.ChecksandBalances.TV, you'll learn how to gather all the facts and make wise financial decisions—what

I call the Checks and Balances approach to personal finance. You'll learn how to dump debt, invest wisely, believe in yourself, and make it happen. The ultimate goal is to achieve the quality of life *you* desire.

What to Expect

I am on a mission to help you succeed in the New Financial Reality. In this book, I will reveal how the financial industry really works, and I'll give you the information, strategies, and tools you need to financially succeed.

Mine is a different approach to personal finance, one that embraces today's new and evolving financial reality with a simple method based on honest assessment and truthful analysis every step of the way.

All the Rules Have Changed begins with helping you figure out what matters most to you—your individual **Quality of Life Factor, or QL Factor.** Once you recognize that as your goal, you can determine how much money you will need to achieve it and how you can go about getting there despite any roadblocks or bumps in the financial road. The QL Factor is different for everyone, as are the personal circumstances that affect the journey and the road you take.

My Checks and Balances approach to personal finance recognizes that and can provide the proper guidance whatever your life stage or circumstance. Whether you're single or married, sandwiched between caring for your children and your own parents, or on your own, you'll learn the right steps to take now.

Checks and Balances Financial Success System™

To succeed in the New Financial Reality you will need to think and act differently. Your financial future is YOUR responsibility. But don't worry. We've designed a system that will help you make critical financial decisions with clarity and confidence. It's as easy as one, two, three... *Know, Check, Act!*

If you *know* the truth by using this book and the information on our website (www.ChecksandBalances.TV), and then implement our step-by-step *check*list process, you can *act* with clarity and confidence.

Financial freedom can be yours. It's not complex, and it is achievable with the Checks and Balances Financial Success System.

3 Steps to Financial Success: Know, Check, Act

KNOW

- Read our FREE, unbiased reports and view our online informational videos to research the facts and discover the truth about almost any product or investment you're thinking of buying.

CHECK

- Download our FREE checklists before you buy any product or investment to become a savvy investor and smarter consumer.

ACT

- With the Checks and Balances Financial Success System, you can move forward rationally and confidently to WIN in the New Financial Reality.

Now You Know

How many times have you said, "If I only knew then- what I know now"? With the Checks and Balances Financial Success System you now have a process to walk you through every financial decision *before* you make that big purchase or investment. You can rest, assured that you have covered all the bases, and can then move forward rationally and confidently to WIN in the New Financial Reality.

Now you have a system to help you make critical financial decisions, and you'll never again have to say, "If I only knew then…" because, *Now You Know!*

PART I

It's Time for Your Financial Wake-up Call

"Reality is not what you wish it to be;
reality is what it really is."

— MATT RETTICK

Chapter 1

Trapped
My Own Journey to Financial Freedom

The middle of winter in central Michigan is tough—biting cold and gray. I didn't think that this particular February night could get more dismal. It was cold outdoors and in. The oil tank in the backyard that provided fuel to heat our one-story home was almost empty—and I didn't have the $400 it would cost to fill it up.

Suddenly my 6-year-old son—at the time we had three children, ages 4, 6, and 10—came running into our bedroom wide-eyed and afraid. "Daddy, Daddy," he cried, "Where's our car? It's gone! Did someone steal it?"

I got up, pulled back the curtain, rubbed the frost off the *inside* of the window and looked out. The car, a four-door Cadillac Seville Brougham with moon roof, leather seats, and all the bells and whistles, was, indeed gone. But I knew it hadn't been stolen.

The car had been top of the line—of course I couldn't afford it. But that hadn't really mattered; I signed my name on the loan anyway. Now I was two and a half months behind in payments—again. In the past when I had missed payments, the lender had threatened to take the car, but the threats had been empty. This dreary night, though, the lender had decided to finally follow through and repossess the vehicle.

Our only car was now gone. I remember that horrible feeling of despair and desperation. There I was, age 27, a husband and father of three young kids living in a rented matchbox house in the middle of winter with no job, no money, and no prospects.

Honestly, I did want to provide for my family. But I was out of get-rich-quick schemes. At that moment, I was ready to give up. This wasn't the first time—or the last—that I felt like throwing in the towel. Actually, I couldn't remember when making ends meet wasn't a struggle.

Life's Lessons Learned Early

My father left us when I was 11 years old, but he was an absentee dad long before that. I would wake up at 4:30 a.m. to struggle through my paper route in suburban Detroit and still get to school on time. Like this February night, those mornings often were dark and frigid, and the feelings of loneliness overwhelming. Riding my bike through the deserted streets, I'd hear a dog bark and be afraid that someone would jump out at me. Back then, I knew that I needed a job to get money. Even then I realized that making money was a tough road. I just hadn't realized how tough.

By the time I was 18, I had quit school to go into business and get rich! "Who needs school?" I figured. I liked having plenty of time to party, and I knew I was going to be a millionaire, no sweat, no problem. I had bought into multi-level-marketing wizard Glenn W. Turner's Koskot Cosmetics distributorship to the tune of $5,000. (I had talked my mother into investing the money.) I had it made! Unfortunately, I had underestimated the challenges on the road to riches. The government soon after shut this cosmetic empire down, and I was left with nothing, including no high school diploma. (That would come later in the form of a GED.)

I've Tried It All

Back to that February night in Pontiac, Michigan. The car was gone. I could do nothing about that. But I had to do something about getting a job. I had to put food on the table and heating oil in the tank. I was used to scrambling and scrounging. To make ends meet, my "career" had advanced from paper route to mucking floors at Dunkin' Donuts, working as a brakeman on the Penn Central Railroad, and beyond. I had tried to peddle everything from Amway products to vacuum sweepers, fire alarms to steaks and seafood, and printing supplies.

At age 24 I was a single father with custody of my two boys who were ages 1 and 2 at the time. In addition to that responsibility, I had child support payments for my daughter, age 4, as well as a cash settlement to my ex-wife. I paid for the boys' babysitter, who eventually became my wife while I worked at a Speedy Printing franchise from 8 a.m. to 6 p.m. six days a week. I had talked my mother into investing her life savings in the franchise, so she supplied the money and I supplied the labor on our joint endeavor. During that time, the kids and I lived on a lot of canned soup and peanut butter and jelly sandwiches. When my mom and I sold the franchise three years later at a slight profit, I was out of a job one more time. I made a little cash on the deal, but instead of using it as an opportunity to get ahead, I burned right through it. I should have invested the proceeds from the Speedy Printing sale and relied on a new job to provide an income stream moving forward. But that was not to be. I hadn't yet wised up to financial reality.

Traveling Salesman With No Car

This time I picked up the newspaper and checked out the all-too-familiar Help Wanted ads. The next day I took yet another sales job, this time selling solar panels for EMG Solar out of Petoskey, Michigan. The only problem was that I was a traveling salesman with no car—and no money to buy one. The pastor of our church took pity on my situation and temporarily loaned me their small church van when I needed it. Two months later I was able to scrape up $600 to buy a well-worn Ford Maverick. It was a far cry from the big dreams of that 18-year-old high school dropout, but I was back on the road to success. Or so I thought at the time. Reality would prove to be far different.

No Instant Riches for Me

We all have read or heard of the self-made billionaire—the Horatio Alger-type hero—who grew up in poverty, swore to get out, and the rest is money-making history. Alas, that was not to be my lot in life. I wish I could say that February night was my wake-up call to get control of my finances and get ahead, but not a chance. I was a long way from that epiphany.

I worked steadily with EMG Solar for six months, and then was promoted to sales trainer. That meant I was finally able to buy a new car—or rather, afford the $2,000 down payment to finance one. I had learned one lesson and rather than take on the steep payments in order to purchase a fancy car, I chose a new Oldsmobile Firenza. It was a compact boxy thing that was no Cadillac. But it was economical and reliable, and my first-ever brand-new vehicle. The smell of the interior reminded me of my accomplishment in overcoming that cold February night. I felt as if I had arrived. Once again, though, I was about to be rudely awakened by reality.

Hopelessly Helpless

Around this time, my Grandma Wick (my mother's mother), whom I adored, had been diagnosed with Alzheimer's disease. Without any financial security for my immediate family, I had to watch helplessly as her mind, body, and finances literally wilted away. What little money she had evaporated quickly because of the care she required. The pain of watching someone I loved lose everything, including her dignity, was horrible.

My father's parents were dealt a similar helpless fate. In 1986, they both moved into a nursing home. My grandmother died about a year later. But my paternal grandfather lived another 12 long years while institutionalized, and, just like with Grandma Wick, I watched him lose everything. It was then that I began to ponder the idea of trying to help others avoid the same financial fate. Not so fast, though. Life wasn't finished throwing me gut-wrenching financial curveballs.

I worked for EMG (still looking for the elusive get-rich-quick scheme) for two years, and then the company cut some of its employees, including me. My next job was with Master Marketing Corporation in Troy, Michigan, where I became an emcee for its sales training events. That meant I rubbed elbows with the mega-giants in motivational speaking—Zig Ziglar, Brian Tracy, Tommy Hopkins, and others. Being around those people motivated me to be like them, and I even wrote my own seven-week sales-training course, which I presented several times to classes of 25 to 30 salespeople each. I sold enrollment in the class, designed the training material, and taught the class.

A Change of Scenery but Not Scenarios

In 1988, finally fed up with Michigan winters, I decided it was time to move somewhere warm—time to think about our quality of life. I quit my job with Master Marketing Corporation and moved my family to Nashville, Tennessee. I didn't know anyone there and didn't have a job, but I loved Tennessee. The weather was great; I liked the people there, too, from the many times we had driven through en route to Florida during what had become our family's regular winter escapes from the Michigan cold. It was Labor Day weekend 1988, and my oldest son had just graduated high school.

Growing up surrounded by the urban concrete jungles of Detroit, I had always wanted to own land—wide open spaces. Tennessee gave me that opportunity. I had sold our Michigan home at a profit, so I bought 12 acres outside of Nashville and began to build a menagerie. (At one point, we had two horses, two cows, 20 chickens, three dogs, and three cats. We've since downsized on the animals.)

I worked at still more get-rich-quick multi-level-marketing schemes, but with much the same dead-end outcome. Like clockwork, I got in over my head yet again when my latest big-money schemes fell apart. I was right back in the familiar territory of that February night in Michigan. I was now two months behind on the mortgage—the lender had threatened foreclosure—two months behind on car payments, and choking on $30,000 in credit-card debt. Old habits and vicious cycles, it seems, die hard.

My Epiphany, Finally

As I mentioned above, one Sunday morning in 1994, I was sitting in church as I did every Sunday, when a woman stood up and loudly began speaking a verse from the Bible. It was Malachi 3:10 (Chapter 3, verse 10; King James Version), and suddenly I truly heard and understood the words for the first time:

"Bring ye all the tithes into the storehouse, that there may be meat in mine house, and prove me now herewith, saith the LORD of hosts, if I

will not open you the windows of heaven, and pour you out a blessing, that there shall not be room enough to receive it."

That was the moment of my financial epiphany—20 years after quitting high school to get rich—and the beginning of my *liberation*. I finally realized—after so many failures—that all my financial woes were the result of being sucked into the "gotta have more stuff to be successful" mentality. In the early years, the "stuff" had been partying and fancy cars. It then evolved into food on the table and a house. A house needs furniture and color TVs, clothes in the closets, dishes in the cupboards, and cars in the driveway. The more I had, the more I wanted. I wanted more stuff than I could really afford, so I used and abused my credit cards. I even made car payments with plastic. I knew better, but that didn't stop me. I figured that if I could make the minimum payment every month, I could have all the stuff I wanted—no sweat, no problem.

Too many of us know where that kind of thinking can and usually does lead. My business slowed down, the economy turned, things happened in life, and it all eventually caught up with me. The walls came crashing down as they always had.

But this time the outcome was different. That Sunday in church I finally saw the light. I got angry for allowing myself to be "duped" into debt, for letting it suck me in and pull me down. I was furious that I had succumbed to the shtick of: "You can have it all, no money down, we'll finance you." My eyes were opened to the truth—I had become a slave to my lenders just as the Bible had cautioned against:

"Owe no man anything, but to love one another: for he that loveth another hath fulfilled the law." —Romans, 13:8 (KJV)

I realized that I was making other people rich while my greed to have it all and have it now made me poor. No more, I vowed. No more buying stuff I didn't need, couldn't afford, and wound up paying for many times over.

Thus began my personal War on Debt! and my awakening to the joy of true financial freedom. You can experience the same kind of liberation and enlightenment.

I may have had an epiphany, but I was still deeply in debt. This time, though, I was on a mission. I was angry, and I resolved to get out there and help myself. I was determined to get out of debt and get a job that led somewhere. I wanted financial security for my family, and I also wanted the opportunity to do what I'd longed to do years ago—help people like my grandparents to be financially prepared for whatever the future might hold. I wanted to help others avoid the financial traps that had snared me and those I loved over and over and over.

I've Done It All, Again

My journey through the financial services industry had begun. It started in 1989 with a job as a health-insurance agent. A few years later, as I studied and learned the business, my work expanded to include helping retirees and pre-retirees with safe money alternatives and estate planning. I became an expert in fixed annuities. My training then extended to more comprehensive planning and investment advice. In 2002, I founded Covenant Reliance Producers (www.CRProducers. com), an insurance marketing organization that educates and supports hundreds of agents across the country. Several years later, I helped put together Brookstone Capital Management (www.BrookstoneCM.com), a registered investment advisory firm. And in 2009, I became a partner in the purchase of Center Street Securities, (www.CenterStreetSecurities.com), a full-service broker/dealer.

Over the years I've learned all the sales pitches and scripts, the ins and outs, pros and cons, fact and fiction, and the biases of nearly every facet of the personal finance and investing business. I understand what it takes to succeed and how financial moves can be doomed to failure. I know the truth, and several years ago I began to clearly see the lies, too.

I've watched stockbrokers sell unsuspecting clients investments they didn't need and shouldn't buy. I've seen annuity salesmen invest all of a client's money into one annuity so that the agent could make a hefty commission. I've seen fee-only financial planners refuse to advise clients to buy an insurance product because a commission was involved. I've listened to talking heads on television and radio give misinformation, bad advice, and sometimes even false facts about a particular investment or insurance product. And I've been disgusted with the multiple scams, con artists, and Ponzi schemes that have destroyed the lives of so many Americans over the last few years. All of this has led me to become "a man on a mission" to inform, educate, and hopefully protect the financial lives of millions of people across our great country.

Yet Another Wake-up Call

Three years ago, I got fed up with it all. That's when I decided it was time for me to make a real difference, to give consumers a fighting chance to achieve their own financial freedom.

As a financial insider, I've lived it, learned it, and done it all. I am here to offer you the truth and the tools you need to financially succeed. It's a powerful feeling to no longer worry about money, even in today's uncertain roller-coaster economy. I want you to experience that feeling. As I teach you how to become a smarter consumer and a savvy investor, you will.

One day after I began to experience and maintain true financial success, my wife told me about the moment when she knew she could finally relax and truly believe we had made it financially. She was at the grocery, and she realized she could buy whatever she wanted to feed the family without worrying that the clerk would have to put something back on the shelf because we didn't have enough money to pay for it. That was my wife's QL moment—her goal achieved.

Years ago when I declared my War on Debt!, the fight was lonely. There was no one I could trust to give me honest and unbiased advice. I didn't have someone at my side who understood my problems and knew the solutions and the pitfalls, someone who had the tools to help me get ahead.

Unlike what I faced back then, you don't have to feel alone in your financial struggles. The Checks and Balances Financial Success System anchored by my Checks and Balances TV show (www.ChecksandBalances.TV) provides you honest and unbiased information backed by my decades of experience and observation in financial services.

With Checks and Balances now you have the opportunity to understand the truth about the economy and investments, and to make the right moves to get your finances and your life on track.

3 Steps to Financial Success: Know, Check, Act

KNOW

- Reality is not what you wish it to be; reality is what it really is!
- The borrower is slave to the lender.

CHECK

- Have you been sucked in by get-rich-quick schemes in the past? What have you learned from your experience?
- Have you been playing the consumer game of buying stuff you don't really need?

ACT

- Move forward with confidence that you can change your financial future.
- Consider applying Malachi 3:10 to your finances and life.
- Discuss what you've learned and felt by reading this chapter with your spouse/significant other.

"You CAN get the true facts and real information you need to make the right financial decisions that can dramatically affect your future."

— MATT RETTICK

Chapter 2

Taking a Stand
The Birth of Checks and Balances TV, Your Source for Balanced Financial Advice

This is an unprecedented time in America's economic history. Our nation is spending money it doesn't have; stock markets are on a giant roller-coaster ride; the real estate bubble has burst; companies that once were strong have needed financial bailouts simply to survive. It's no wonder consumers have lost confidence—and cash—for the future. Yet despite this New Financial Reality fraught with uncertainty swirling around markets and marketplaces, jobs and security, each of us still has the opportunity to achieve our dreams and goals *if* we take control of our financial lives today and plan accordingly.

When I set out on my journey to financial freedom, I didn't have any resources to help me make sense of the facts, figures, and financial fantasies that then (and even more so now) bombarded my brain. Even after I became an expert in the financial services industry, with more than two decades of helping thousands of people, I recognized that not everyone gets the honest assessments and plain information they need to make the right financial decisions.

> **Financial freedom:** *A state of life in which you have enough money to do what's important to you without worrying about the cost.*

The Checks and Balances Beginnings

Three years ago I finally had had enough with all the bias, misinformation, and self-serving hype. I was tired of seeing and hearing about consumers and clients misled by inadequate and often inaccurate investing and retirement advice. I decided Americans deserved a better chance to find their financial freedom. After all, how can you make the right financial moves without a clear understanding of how money and financial products really work?

The answer is: You can't. Each of us needs to understand how today's economic changes do or do not impact our personal finances. Only then can we determine the right moves to help realize our financial dreams.

I decided to do something to help people access the information they need. That's when Checks and Balances TV (www.ChecksandBalances .TV) was born. It's designed as your online information center that gives you facts, unbiased perspective, pluses and minuses, and the inside information you need to make confident, informed decisions about your money and your life.

No matter what you hear, there are two sides to every topic. Money matters are no exception. Checks and Balances provides you the straight talk on both sides—the pros and cons and everything in-between—when it comes to current events and financial topics, insights, and advice. We've deliberately designed the site as a place where you can check the facts and balance the information to better understand what the current financial headlines really mean. The real facts about money are a simple click away, anytime, anywhere, online 24/7.

WHAT'S ON CBTV?

- Get the real truth about current financial and economic events with the help of straight-forward balanced financial analysis, insights, and direction.

- Learn if and how those current events affect you now and in the future.

- Get the scoop on how you, too, can become a 21st century investor with the help of valuable and enduring financial tips that can help you grow, protect, and preserve your nest egg.

- Download free reports and how-to guides on relevant financial topics.

- Access and download valuable, customizable documents essential to getting your own financial house in order.

- Watch free, archived audio and video podcasts of Checks and Balances TV shows as well as important interviews to keep you informed, up-to-date, and on track financially.

What's So Important About the Right Information?

Plenty of people get caught up in what they believe are "guaranteed" tickets to wealth, "get-rich-quick schemes," and "proprietary investments" to secure their future. If you doubt that, look at the financial playing field these days. It's littered with individuals—from all walks of life—who listened to the hype on television, radio, or from some smooth-talking scammer, and then believed they were on the road to riches, only to end up losing a chunk of their cash, if not their entire life savings. Chances are most of us know someone who had to postpone retirement or was pushed back into the workforce because their finances came up short. I'm not talking about big risk-takers, either. These are regular people like you who likely listened to some too-good-to-be-true deal and who did what they thought was right with their money. Unfortunately, far too many of their plans and financial investments turned out to be all wrong.

Who hasn't heard of tragic case after tragic case of the elderly man or woman who lost everything, including his or her dignity, because he or she didn't adequately plan for their later years? It's degrading and an outrage that people who worked all their lives should end up without any money, dependent on the government, or fading away in a nursing home. As mentioned earlier, I watched in horror as that fate befell my father's parents. My maternal grandmother, who suffered from Alzheimer's, hadn't planned financially for her future either. She didn't end up in a nursing home, but I watched the agony my aunt went through taking care of her. Those are experiences that helped inspire me to start CBTV.

These scenarios are all too common, and will become more so as the New Financial Reality derails many more ill-prepared Americans. My goal is to educate you so you are in control of your own destiny.

How Checks and Balances Can Make a Difference

Nearly every week, headlines are filled with news of unsuspecting consumers talked into investing in a concept or giving money to a financial products salesman only to be scammed. The most well-known of those scams involved New York stockbroker and money manager Bernie Madoff, who conned thousands of people out of billions of dollars in the largest Ponzi scheme in history. As I'm sure you know by now, Madoff is serving a life sentence—150 years—in prison. His investors, however, can take little solace in that. His investors ended up losing most of their investment—or entire life savings, in many cases—and now are just out of luck.

Securities fraud happens all the time on a much smaller scale. That's one of the reasons why our government and private industry have put into place accounting standards, fraud investigation units, and securities regulators. In an ideal world, such safeguards would prevent bad financial things from happening to good people. But they don't. Budget crunches, politics, and staff cutbacks aside, regulations are man-made and regulators are human. Mistakes are made, and problems ignored or overlooked. Years before Madoff was snared, the Securities and Exchange Commission investigated his dealings several times without finding anything wrong!

The Big Financial Lie

The financial system that we all have grown up with is based on what I call "The Big Financial Lie." The financial services industry, like most other industries, wants to make a profit. But unfortunately, that profit can come at your expense. You must be careful that you don't end up with something that isn't right for you. It's always good to remember that the financial system usually makes money whether you do or not.

We've been inundated with marketing ploys for so long that we buy "stuff" without realizing that these products exist to make profits for the company selling them. Home-equity firms, credit-card companies, auto companies, and mortgage companies—to name a few—base their efforts on a system that keeps their profits flowing while keeping us in financial bondage, sometimes throughout our entire lives.

Among the biggest lies:

- **Big credit-card debt is fine as long as you make the minimum payment.** The truth is that unless you pay off your credit-card balance monthly, you are being sucked into crippling, long-term debt with exorbitant interest rates and all types of fees for late payments, bounced checks, and more. That $50 dinner can end up costing hundreds instead.

- **Stockbrokers and insurance agents always work in your best interests.** The truth is that some stockbrokers and insurance agents are simply salespeople selling a product to generate a commission or fee.

- **Brokerage houses work hard to develop investment strategies tailored to individual clients' needs.** The truth is that financial and investment "strategies" sometimes are a one-size-fits-all approach.

- **Now you can have the car of your dreams for no money down and low monthly payments.** Car dealers are notorious for enticing us because of our greed, and selling us automobiles that tie us to monthly payments that last five to seven years. If you try to sell the car in the first three to four years, you often end up owing more than the vehicle's worth!

- **Wall Street is the place to put most of your money if you want big returns over time.** The underlying premise here is that Wall Street will make you rich. The truth is there's never a guarantee. Wall Street can end up becoming a frustrating way to lose money over time.

Over the past several years of roller-coaster markets and a struggling economy, I'll bet you've likely heard at least one or two of the following comments from a stockbroker or advisor, and all are poor excuses for inadequate investment advice and direction:

- Hang in there; the market always comes back.

- It's only a paper loss.

- The markets have averaged double-digit returns since 1926.

- When the market goes down, that's good. Dollar-cost-averaging is working for you if you keep investing money monthly.

- Past performance is no guarantee of future earnings.

The Value of Becoming an Educated Consumer

We all must learn to recognize the two sides to every investment or purchase. That sounds simple enough, but it isn't necessarily an easy concept to put into practice.

Chasing greed doesn't have to be of Madoff proportions, either. Stock price manipulation happens all the time, and if you're a small investor, you generally lose because you either ignore the warning signs or are unaware of them. Checks and Balances puts you in control, instead.

Reality Check

Doubling your money in five years might have been a "conditioned reality" in the heady days before the Internet or real estate bubbles burst. But looking to double your money in a relatively short time is not a solid long-term strategy. The financial markets' meltdown and collapsed housing markets have proven that. Sure, it's possible to find the single gem that truly may shine over the long term. But you can't count on the stock market to do it all for you. Your financial future depends on other important financial strategies as well.

> *The quickest way to double your money today is to*
> *fold it in half and put it back in your pocket!*

The security of your finances today and tomorrow depends on whether you get real and get it right for the long term. That's what the true experts mean when they emphasize making sure an investment's fundamentals are solid.

Learning to Hear the Truth

As with every other decision we make in our lives, when it comes to money we need to start with the truth—with the unbiased and factual pros and cons. Yet you don't always get the whole truth about potential investments or strategic approaches to long-term investing. Experience as an investor, advisor, and teacher has taught me that.

It's not that sellers of products or sources of information purposely mislead or intend to scam you. It's simply human nature that someone pitching a product will likely have inherent or subconscious biases when presenting purchase options. Those blind spots mean that you don't get the whole truth regarding an investment, a major purchase, or a specific approach to money management.

Bias is part of being human. You must train yourself to pay attention to that and to factor bias into what you hear, see, and read. That goes for money matters, too. Even family members, friends, and co-workers are biased. They may not be selling anything, but the bias exists.

My Mission

For every expert or statistic that says one thing, there's likely a statistic and expert to support the opposite approach—particularly when investments and money are involved. I am on a mission to help you sift through the information that is available and avoid the heartache, heartbreak, hardships, and horrors that I experienced and later observed regarding money.

> *"There are three kinds of lies: lies, damned lies, and statistics."* —Mark Twain

I care because I've been there and I understand the pain. I am committed to creating public awareness on topics that need to be addressed and understood. I am committed to helping you gain your financial freedom. As a retirement advisor and expert in personal finance, I understand the challenges we all face. I am here with the answers to your money questions. I want you to learn from my experiences.

Why is my approach different? It's different because it shows you how to focus on financial reality and not get derailed. Checks and Balances is your source for balanced financial advice, for the truth about money and money matters. If you know the pros and cons, positives and negatives of today's financial issues and investments, you now have a fighting chance to achieve your financial freedom. CBTV puts you in the driver's seat.

You have a responsibility to investigate the facts yourself, balance both sides of an issue, investment, or purchase, and then make a decision that's best for your individual situation. Checks and Balances helps you do that.

3 Steps to Financial Success: Know, Check, Act

KNOW

- Financial freedom is a state of life in which you have enough money to do what's important to you without worrying about the cost.

- Be aware of The Big Financial Lie.

- The quickest way to double your money today is to fold it in half and put it back in your pocket!

CHECK

- Become an educated investor by asking a lot of questions and researching the company and/or advisor you're considering.

- Download our free reports and checklists to learn the "insider" information you need to make good financial decisions.

ACT

- Move cautiously before investing your hard-earned money into any investment or product.

- Saying "no" to 10 good investments is better than saying "yes" to just one bad investment.

"Life is not fair. What makes it fair is that it's not fair to everyone."

— MATT RETTICK

Chapter 3

Fasten Your Seatbelt
The New Financial Reality Has Arrived

Today's New Financial Reality seriously threatens your future unless you wake up to it, take control of it, and act now. Traditional approaches to money, credit, and personal finance aren't good enough anymore. In this new reality, job and retirement security is gone. Many of us face new and broader responsibilities as part of the country's changing demographics.

To thrive today requires new approaches and a different attitude toward money. It's time to forget the mentality that greed is good, put aside the false hopes and promises of easy riches and fast credit, and make the right financial moves to ensure *your* future and the future of *your* money.

Face the Truth

Now it's your time to face the hard truth about money in your life:

- You're probably not going to get rich. (You may, but don't pin your happiness on it.)

- You aren't going to win the mega-jackpot lottery.

- Chances are a rich relative won't leave you a fortune.

- You're not likely to strike it rich by getting in on the ground floor of the next Apple, Intel, or Microsoft.

33

And, in case you're banking on cashing in at craps or the blackjack table in Las Vegas, that isn't going to happen. No matter what the advertisements and hype claims, chasing greed seldom works out in your favor. Racking up $10,000, $20,000, or even $40,000 or more in credit-card debt to "keep up with the Joneses" is not OK either.

Neither can you count on the government or anyone else to take care of you. The same-employer-for-life scenario is gone. Corporate pensions often are underfunded or nonexistent. Social Security and Medicare have their own challenges. Meanwhile, health-insurance costs, including out-of-your-pocket expenses, continue to soar. Unfortunately, maxed-out credit and over-mortgaged homes are common. You can no longer rely on your home's equity to finance your retirement. Savings are virtually nil for many people, too.

THE NEW FINANCIAL REALITY

Each of us must face the stark facts when it comes to planning for our retirement:

- Americans are living longer, which means your money has to last longer, too.

- The cost of health care continues to spiral upward with no end in sight.

- You can't count on government entitlement programs to finance your retirement.

- Employment for life with accompanying pension and health-care security are no longer the norm.

- With uncertainties in housing markets, you can't count on financing your retirement with your home's equity, either.

New Economics

Don't despair, though. The New Financial Reality is not the economic chaos that some people would have you believe. It does require, however, that you think differently. Making ends meet, for starters, and ultimately thriving and achieving your dreams require a determined mindset and a consumer-savvy approach to money.

RETIREMENT IN TROUBLE

Americans' confidence in their ability to afford a comfortable retirement remains at historic lows, according to the 2012 Retirement Confidence Survey from the nonprofit, nonpartisan Employee Benefit Research Institute.

- 47 percent of American workers worry whether they will have a comfortable retirement.

- 46 percent worry about having enough money to pay for health care in retirement.

- 60 percent say the total value of their household's savings and investments, excluding the value of their primary home and defined benefit plans, is less than $25,000.

Source: www.ebri.org/surveys/rcs/2012/

Adding to the confusion of this new reality are major changes in what traditionally has been considered "the norm." Consider some of what's different today.

The "Leave It to Beaver" family is no more. Adult parents find themselves financially squeezed by their grown children and their own aging parents; grandparents end up being responsible for their grandchildren (I can relate to that!). Marriage is at an all-time low. ("America's Families and Living Arrangement: 2011," U.S. Census press release, Nov. 3, 2011; www.census.gov/newsroom/releases/archives/families_households/cb11-183.html.)

Our economic base has changed. Gone is the job-for-life-and-then-retire scenario. Stability has been replaced by entrepreneurial small businesses and job—and paycheck—insecurities. Small businesses represent 99.7 percent of all employer firms and have generated 65 percent of the net new jobs over the past 17 years (www.sba.gov/sites/default/files/sbfaq.pdf).

The concept of retirement has evolved. Retirement benefits through an employer are fast becoming extinct. Defined-benefit plans are disappearing, and Social Security and Medicare are big unknowns for the future. In other words, it's up to you to take care of your own retirement.

Health-care costs have spiraled out of control. Families often can't afford health insurance or health care, and neither can singles, seniors, nor retirees.

People are living longer. That means your money has to last longer, too. When the Social Security System was established in 1935, the average life expectancy was just over 61 years. People were expected to retire and collect Social Security for perhaps a few years, if that. As of 2010, the average life expectancy had climbed to more than 78 years (www.cdc.gov/nchs/fastats/lifexpec.htm; www.cdc.gov/nchs/data/nvsr58/nvsr58_21.pdf; www.ssa.gov/policy/docs/ssb/v49n10/v49n10p24.pdf).

New Approach

In this New Financial Reality, each of us needs to rethink how money relates to our lives. We need to examine our personal responsibilities, whether that means learning to stretch a paycheck, hoarding a nest egg, or reviving a gasping retirement plan. Maybe it means discovering what it takes in today's economy to hold onto mad money, protect investments (big and small), or keep up payments on an upside-down mortgage. Or maybe—like most people—you must deal with a combination of scenarios and responsibilities complicated further by all the "noise" out there.

Each of us also must sort through the misinformation and learn to recognize what it is we really need vs. what we think we want, and then make well-researched financial choices. Only by taking responsibility for our own financial reality will we be able to enjoy what's meaningful and purposeful in our lives.

Beyond the Money

Money troubles can reach far beyond your finances. They can hurt your marriage and your health, too. In a 2011 online poll, 27 percent of more than 1,400 respondents indicated that their marriage was experiencing the most stress as a result of their financial situation, while 24 percent said their health was suffering, according to the National Foundation for Credit Counseling, a national nonprofit credit counseling agency (http://www.nfcc.org/Newsroom/newsreleases/FinancialDistress.cfm).

The Checks and Balances Action Plan

Life is a do-it-yourself program complicated by outside pressures and this New Financial Reality. To successfully cope, you must develop mental and physical plans of action based on what's real and true about your circumstances.

Most important, though, we must take action. Whatever your age, you can achieve financial freedom. You can create your own path to financial independence that allows you to live the life you envision on your own terms. Even if you're buried in debt, behind in savings, or weighed down with responsibilities, you can reach your goals of being debt free and financially independent. Remember, I've lived through it all, so I know what it takes to do it.

The Quality of Life Factor

What matters most to you in life? I call that your Quality of Life Factor (QL). It can and often does have very little to do with being rich and lots to do with being independent and happy. Achieving your QL should be a big part of your long-term financial goal. Taking control of your financial life, after all, no longer is about buying or selling investments or other products you don't want or need, or pursuing goals—financial or otherwise—that don't really matter to you. Your personal financial reality should be about making the right financial moves today to get where you truly want to be tomorrow.

> *Your Quality of Life Factor likely has little to do with being rich beyond your wildest dreams, and lots to do with being independent.*

Your success should be about creating a life that brings you contentment. You don't have to achieve someone else's version of success to be happy. In fact, that's a recipe for disaster and disappointment.

You may have aspirations for a QL that requires lots of money or one that doesn't. Whatever you decide as your QL, it's *your* choice. Achieving it is up to you, too. We'll work on defining your own QL in Chapter 4 and then work on achieving it in subsequent chapters.

Basis in Financial Truths

You can have the financial wherewithal you need to achieve your happiness, no matter your current circumstances. I've come a long way from that bleak February night in central Michigan and have overcome plenty of odds. You can beat the odds, too.

Once you understand and accept this reality, you are on your way. In the ups and downs of life and finances, we often easily forget the lessons (and truths) we learn and fall back into the same old habits. It took me years on the financial roller coaster of life to realize that. But once I did, my life—financial and otherwise—began to turn around.

Reality Check for All of Us

Unfortunately, much financial advice still seems to take the one-size-fits-all approach so commonly accepted in the past. Today's financial landscape, however, looks nothing like that of years past.

The Small Business/Self-Employed Conundrum

Not everyone works as an employee of a big corporation anymore. Maybe that full-time corporate employee complete with full-time everything-you-ever-wanted-or-needed benefits was the case yesterday, but not so in the New Financial Reality. Small businesses and the self-employed account for a big chunk of today's U.S. workforce.

How big a workforce is involved? As of December 2012, nearly 9.7 million Americans were self-employed (www.bls.gov/news.release/pdf/empsit.pdf). That means many workers don't enjoy the perks or benefits of the corporate lifestyle. The financial security of matching 401(k) contributions and health or disability insurance simply doesn't exist for them. The U.S. Small Business Administration estimates that 99.7 percent of all employer firms are small businesses, and that those firms accounted for 65 percent of the net new jobs over the last 17 years (www.sba.gov/sites/default/files/FAQ_Sept_2012.pdf).

That's a changing workforce. What might be a sound financial move for a corporate employee isn't necessarily so for someone who is self-employed, and vice versa. Talking about 401(k) retirement plans and employer-matching funds means absolutely nothing to someone who is self-employed. Instead, they think in terms of SEP-IRAs, IRAs, and other personal savings options.

When it comes to health insurance, corporate employees might complain about paying a few hundred dollars a month for coverage, while the self-employed face out-of-pocket expenses that can run into thousands of dollars a year. That's if a small business or self-employed person can afford health insurance at all.

Changing Demographics

Unmarried couples account for a growing segment of the population, too. Barely half of all U.S. adults are married today. That compares with 72 percent of adults ages 18 and older who had tied the knot in 1960 (Pew Research Center, analysis of U.S. Census data (www.pewsocialtrends. org/2011/12/14/barely-half-of-u-s-adults-are-married-a-record-low/).

Even more indicative of our changing demographics, married couples with adult children today find themselves footing the bills for those kids well into their adult lives. Nearly 60 percent of parents today provide financial support for their adult children (online poll by Harris Interactive for the National Endowment for Financial Education and in cooperation with Forbes.com (www. nefe. org/press-room/news/parents-financially-supporting-adult-children.aspx).

Your Part in the New Financial Reality

Think none of this applies to you? That's what I thought long after the kids were grown and I had achieved financial stability and success. Then we received a telephone call late one night. It was a February again! One of our sons was on the phone telling us that he and his wife had split. He had quit his job, and he was driving their three very young children from their home in Florida to us in Tennessee. He asked for our help raising his kids until he got on his feet again.

In those few minutes, our life changed. We knew we had to immediately get custody of the children. One minute we were long-distance grandparents, then suddenly we were raising young kids all over again. I promise you, that wasn't something I had planned or prepared for!

It happened a second time, too, a number of years later with the same three grandchildren. So, don't ever assume that it absolutely won't happen to you.

What the Statistics Really Mean

All of us regularly are inundated with the "latest statistics" on whatever is the financial topic of the moment—new home starts, unemployment rates, business failures, the consumer price index, and daily industrial average or S&P 500. Along with the ever-changing statistics come the endless "analysis" and "must" financial moves of the day from the "in-the-know" experts of the moment. Some of it makes sense sometimes; some of it doesn't.

Many of the comments may have some basis in fact, but the source of the analysis often has a vested interest in selling you something—advice included. The direct effect of the statistic on you and your finances often is minimal, if there's any effect at all. Sound financial investments, after all, should involve a balanced, long-term approach to handling your money.

Yet all these numbers and analyses do point to legitimate concern about the financial future of our country and beyond. The economy isn't really getting much better very quickly. That means getting the most bang for your buck these days is essential, especially in inflationary economic times.

You need to separate financial fact from fiction when being besieged by repeated statistics and the accompanying flurry of "must-move-now" advice.

Checks and Balances Tools

For more on understanding the news and its effect on your money, download or read today's financial headlines and free reports at www.ChecksandBalances.TV:

- Financial Fact or Fiction?
- 21st Century Investing
- Debt-Free Retirement
- Financial Freedom Wake-up Call
- Financial Freedom Personal Check-up

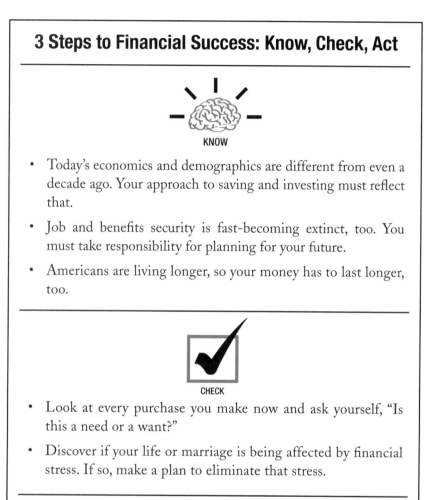

3 Steps to Financial Success: Know, Check, Act

KNOW

- Today's economics and demographics are different from even a decade ago. Your approach to saving and investing must reflect that.

- Job and benefits security is fast-becoming extinct, too. You must take responsibility for planning for your future.

- Americans are living longer, so your money has to last longer, too.

CHECK

- Look at every purchase you make now and ask yourself, "Is this a need or a want?"

- Discover if your life or marriage is being affected by financial stress. If so, make a plan to eliminate that stress.

ACT

- Your success—or failure—to achieve what truly matters to you is up to you. It's your choice, not the choice of your financial advisor, your parents, your neighbor, or your employer.

- Tune out the daily, weekly, and monthly "latest" gyrations of the stock market and the analysis along with it. If you've done your homework and invested thoughtfully, these numbers have little day-to-day effect on your long-term financial goals.

"Life is a do-it-to-yourself program. Your success or failure is up to the man or woman in the mirror."

— MATT RETTICK

Chapter 4

Stop Playing the Game
Discover Your Quality of Life Factor

No matter the obstacles you face or the responsibilities that weigh you down, it's up to you to choose financial freedom.

It's time to face the real facts, balance the choices, and then rely on yourself to create and build your ideal financial future. With the unvarnished facts and honest, unbiased direction, and with the help of a true financial advisor, you can do it. It takes a true financial advisor to help you in your quest because there's simply too much that you must know and understand to go it all on your own.

A true financial advisor is someone who takes a holistic approach to your financial planning needs and who has only your best interests and your financial success at heart. He or she can provide comprehensive, all-inclusive solutions that utilize diverse products and strategies to meet your specific needs.

It's Your Turn

Your journey to financial freedom starts with a jolt. It's the "aha!" moment when you realize it's time to take control of your personal finances and truly change your life for the better.

This wake-up call can come at different ages and stages of your life. Because old money habits die hard, one wake-up call isn't always enough, either. Some people may never experience the "aha!" moment despite mountains of debt and the prospect of poverty in their future.

Your "aha!" could come during time spent with a dying parent or loved one—perhaps a promise made to get control of your money. Or, enlightenment might strike when the stark reality of your financial situation—things like bankruptcy, divorce, home foreclosure, auto repossession, and more—finally and inescapably hits you.

As I mentioned in Chapter 1, my revelation was in church where I had spent literally thousands of other moments reading and repeating similar words. This time, as debilitating debt yet again threatened me and my family, those biblical words from Malachi 3:10 hit home. I realized that I had become trapped in an endless cycle of "buy more now and pay it off later," but I never paid it off. I saw that I had become a slave to the credit companies and allowed them to control my life. That made me mad enough to do something about it—to launch me on my journey to financial freedom. And, it was time to put God first.

As you know by now, that wasn't my first "aha!" moment. My journey to financial freedom actually involved several jolts along the way. That's what it takes for some of us, especially when we don't have access to honest, reliable, and unbiased guidance. Up until that momentous day in church, however, none of the jolts had been strong enough to dislodge me from what had become my tragic boom/bust financial cycle.

Importance of Purpose

My first jolt came when I was 18. After quitting high school short of my diploma and failing in the first of many attempts to get rich quick, I was at a party where everyone was drinking and having a good time. I leaned up against the wall and slid down to sit with my buddies on the floor. A couple of them were former track team standouts and were reminiscing about the "good old days in high school." These high-school dropouts—like me—had no prospects, no real future, nothing beyond reliving past glories. At that moment a few of the clouds parted in my party-dazed brain and I realized that I was 18, wasting my life, and going nowhere. I had quit school to party life away instead of doing something purposeful.

I literally dragged myself up, went home, and got sober. Shortly afterward, I earned my high school GED—general equivalency diploma—and then found a real job as a custodian at Dunkin' Donuts. It was hard work and not what I planned to do the rest of my life, but it had a purpose and set me on my way. When I quit a few months later to work for the Pennsylvania Central Railroad—yet another chapter on my long journey—my boss was sorry to see me go. He said I was the best custodian he'd ever had.

The unfortunate reality is that when it comes to money, few of us know what we truly want or how to achieve it. As a young man and long before I learned the financial services business, I certainly didn't. Sadly, most people find themselves in similar situations. They don't know how to interpret economic events and how or if those events affect them personally. They don't know what to do with their money and why to choose or discard one financial option over another. They don't know how to get started, so they just keep procrastinating.

Concepts like the value of compounding interest as a tool to grow your investments, life insurance as a flexible savings vehicle, or investments with security of principal built in all are foreign. Unfortunately, too, few people understand how to ensure that they and their loved ones will be financially secure tomorrow as well as today with the help of the right insurance, investments, and planning. We are bombarded with biased options and self-serving sales pitches. We're taught to do what everyone says we should do even though it makes little sense for our own lives.

Your Quality of Life Factor

Forget for a moment what others say should be your aspirations in life, all those things you're conditioned to think should be your long-term goals—bigger house, newer car, fancier clothes, the newest electronic gadget. Instead, try to envision the future you truly would like to have. What would satisfy you and make you happy? What is your personal Quality of Life Factor (QL)? Is it, as I once thought, a fancy car like that Cadillac Seville Brougham? Suppose you achieve that shiny goal. Even if you could afford it, how long will that car satisfy you? Will you need to get a better and newer car next year?

Or does your happiness lie closer to home? Maybe it involves your relationships with friends and family. Maybe it's the pursuit of a vocation or avocation that you find rewarding in itself, apart from whatever money or prestige it brings you.

You need to determine for yourself what makes you happy. It's your call, not that of your parents, teachers, preacher, friends, or family. It shouldn't depend on the current size of your investment portfolio, either. Achieving your QL is entirely up to you and completely within your control. After all, that's what the New Financial Reality is all about—your ability to achieve your dreams and satisfy your needs. Let's look more closely at how you can recognize your own true QL.

Face the Facts

You're probably never going to have it all—the yachts, the Lamborghinis, the multiple mansions, the private jets, and the ability to travel anywhere at anytime. That doesn't mean, though, you can't have all you need and then some. You can take that annual Mediterranean cruise if that's part of your dream. You can own that dynamite sports car, live in your dream home, retire comfortably and happily, send your children and grandchildren to college, help that charitable cause that's dear to you, and even leave a nest egg for future generations. You simply must learn to make the right financial decisions. Your finances don't have to dictate your future happiness, but they will if you don't make the right choices now.

Those choices begin with understanding what matters most to you— your QL. That QL can change, too, as your life circumstances change. What was important to you at age 20 will probably change in your 30s, 40s, 50s, and beyond. Today my financial circumstances have changed for the better. My QL has shifted from making enough money to pay the bills and put food on the table to making sure I use my talents and expertise to help others achieve their dreams and goals, and to find their QL.

Understanding What Makes Up Your QL

Quality of Life Factor means many different things to many people— from your faith and how you may choose to serve God to your dreams, experiences, and even material goods, if that's what truly matters. The foundation of a QL, though, is the same for everyone. It's based on happiness: What is it that truly makes you happy? Once you know the answer to that question, you can chart a course that will provide the finances to achieve your happiness and, in turn, the security of knowing you will achieve that happiness.

> *"Your wealth is in your time, not your money."* —Matt Rettick

All this may sound a bit too ethereal and abstract for a book about money, but happiness is the basis for what we do with our money, whether in our lives or the lives of others. That's what gratification—instant or otherwise—is all about. We buy things for gratification; we plan our lives for gratification. We want to be happy, and we want those we love to be happy. The right kind of financial security can help us achieve that happiness.

Your Goals and Your Dreams

Now it's your turn to examine your goals and dreams, to be honest with yourself and think about what matters most to you. What is it that will truly make you happy? I'm not talking about the instant gratification you get from buying a 72-inch TV or snagging tickets to next year's Super Bowl. This is serious and life-changing. What if you learned you were going to die in six months? What is it that would allow you to die happy? It could very well be attending the Super Bowl in style. But the bottom line is that, instead, it could be making sure that your loved ones are financially cared for after you're gone, or something else entirely that is just as uniquely your key to happiness.

Shortly before Apple co-founder Stephen Jobs died in 2011 at age 56, he lamented that he hadn't spent more time with his family. Here's a man with more money than he could ever spend and all the professional accomplishments he could ever want, yet his one regret was that he hadn't spent enough time with his family. That time with loved ones was his *true* QL.

A good friend and business associate used to work 24/7. He was driven to get ahead—far ahead—financially. He lived and breathed his company, and did very well financially. Then one day he had a massive wake-up call. While teaching a training class for financial advisors, he became short of breath, light-headed, and lost his voice. Concerned, he went to the hospital emergency room where they discovered he had an aneurism ready to burst.

My friend immediately was rushed into surgery. Twice during the nine-hour operation the doctors came out to tell his wife he was near death. Miraculously, though, he pulled through.

After that near-death experience, my friend was a changed man. He put his life in perspective. Today he works far less, spends lots of time with his family, and truly lives his QL.

Perhaps, like my friend or like Jobs, your QL is being able to spend extended quality time with your family and having the financial security to do that. Or, maybe you're single or widowed and have always dreamed of being able to cruise the world. A QL, too, could revolve around pursuit of knowledge or involve global volunteer work. Whatever it is that will bring you happiness is what makes up your QL.

When I lived in Pontiac, Michigan, I was a member of the choir in our church, Williams Lake Church of the Nazarene. One of my fellow choir members, Max, and his wife used to go to South America every year on what the church called "work and witness mission trips." The group would spend two weeks—usually in poor, remote villages—building churches.

Max regularly would ask me to come along, but I was always too busy making money. Frankly, I also couldn't understand the attraction of spending a vacation doing back-breaking, dirty work in the hot sun in a dusty Third World country.

I finally asked Max why he went every year. His response was unexpected. "My wife and I haven't taken a traditional vacation in years. But what we get out of the mission trip is so much more than going to a beach for a couple of weeks."

Suddenly, I got it! Since then, I have been fortunate enough to join the trips, too. One year I went to Santa Cruz, Bolivia, where we helped build a two-story church. Another year, I helped build a church in Lima, Peru. You think you're going to serve these poor people, who have nothing, by building a church. What happens instead, is that they serve you with wonderful smiles, boundless food, and joyous entertainment. The people of the villages simply overflow with gratitude that you chose to come to their community to help them.

Your LifeCheck

Understanding what matters most to you in life—your QL—must begin with an assessment of where you are now, what you have and don't have today, and what you would like to have tomorrow. Sure, we all want to be free of money worries and able to buy whatever we want, but this is a much deeper assessment of what matters to you. It's back to the question of what would allow you to die happy if you had only six months to live. My guess is it wouldn't be having a million dollars in the bank.

Start with the following simple exercise:

What matters most to you?

Rate on a scale of 1 to 10 (1 being least happy and 10 being the happiest) your degree of happiness now, and in an ideal world, when it comes to:

	Now	Ideal World
Family life		
Wealth		
Health		
Sports activities		
Fulfilling my purpose in life		
Enjoying my work		
Laughter at home		
Meaningful personal relationships		
Active faith		
Volunteering/Helping others		
Travel		
Enjoying the arts		
Other		
TOTALS		

After you've completed the exercise, look at your answers. In which topic or topics did you score highest? Which did you assign the lowest score? If you're honest in your assessments, you'll begin to see a pattern in what brings you the most happiness today and likely will do so in the future. Your QL should relate to that pattern. Dig deeper within that particular category or categories and ask yourself what would truly bring you contentment in the future.

YOUR LIFECHECK QUIZ

What is your level of happiness today? To get a better idea, ask yourself the following questions. Be honest in your responses, and keep in mind that there are no right or wrong answers. This is simply a way to help you realize the importance of where you stand in today's financial reality.

- Do you enjoy what you're doing at work? At home? In your free time?

- Do you work to live or live to work? In other words, do you find yourself giving up activities you enjoy in your free time to take care of work matters?

- What or who controls your life? (If you don't know the answer to that, ask yourself where or how you spend most of your time.)

- Do you live paycheck to paycheck or do you have extra cash at the end of each month?

- If you're out of cash at the end of the month, is it because you spent the money on staples like food and shelter, or did you buy other things, too?

- Are you always buying more stuff? Why or why not? If so, what kind of stuff?

- If you didn't have to worry about money, what would you love to do with your life?

Balance and a Quality of Life

ASSESSING YOUR LIFE

Some questions to consider when looking at your own QL:

- Is your personal life in balance?
- Are you prepared for a worst-case scenario?
- Have you planned for the future?
- Is your debt under control?

Don't overlook the importance of balance in your life. We often make decisions, especially when finances are involved, that fall short on satisfaction because they overlook the role of balance in our lives. My friend thought work was everything until he almost died, and then he realized life was so much more.

I would like the words on my tombstone to say:
"He looked for the best in others and gave the
*best he had." —*Matt Rettick

Answering the following questions should help show you that your true QL likely involves more than dreams. It's about balance, too, especially when money and security are involved.

Is Your Personal Life in Balance?

How balanced is your personal life? We've all heard the clichés, "Life is too short" or "There's simply not enough time in life." Nonetheless, at one time or another we've all been guilty of saying, "Not now. I'm too busy. Today I have to..." You fill in the blank with whatever crisis of the moment is distracting you from living a truly balanced life.

Let's approach it another way. After you die, what will be your epitaph? Will it be, "A great worker lies here"? Or would you rather the words be something more meaningful? If whatever you're doing is not leading toward a meaningful life that you'll look back on with satisfaction, change

51

course now! Make a conscious decision to make the important things in your life your highest priority.

Life truly isn't about money or investments or 72-inch TVs. What matters most in life are the people you love and care about, and who love and care about you.

Now again ask yourself, "Is my personal life in balance?"

Expect the Best, But Be Prepared for the Worst

- *What would happen if the absolute worst-case scenario occurred in your life today?* A mentor taught me that if I can live with that worst-possible scenario, everything else will take care of itself. What is your worst-case scenario?

- *What if you died tomorrow?* Do you have family or loved ones depending on you? Are you married with a spouse who has no independent income? If you were gone, would she or he be financially secure? Could they make it without you?

- *Are you retired?* Would your spouse lose Social Security income or a pension if you suddenly were gone? If you're not married, what would happen to your partner or loved one? Could he or she afford to go on? Do you or your partner have children or dependents? Do you have life insurance with the proper documentation that would allow those dependents to keep living the way you and your income have allowed them to live?

- *What if you lost your job?* Do you have contingency plans in place that allow you and your loved ones to continue financially until you can secure another job?

- *What if you were in a serious automobile accident?* If you could never work again, how would you pay your bills? Or, if you were working at home and perhaps fell off the roof and were injured to the point you were out of work for months, do you have a plan in place that would provide cash for you and your loved ones to live on?

Such scenarios figure into your QL. And, there's more.

Am I Planning for the Future?

Are you planning for the future or living for the moment? When I was a kid delivering newspapers in Michigan, I very badly wanted to go on my ninth-grade class trip to Washington, D.C. The trip, including airfare, meals, and hotels, cost $299 (yes, it was a long time ago!). Early in the school year, I came home with the details and anxiously asked my single mom if she would send me.

My mother couldn't afford to do that, but she said she would "help me" save for the trip. She took out a calendar and a piece of paper and divided the cost of the trip by the number of weeks until the trip. Then she made a chart that showed how much I would have to earn each week between now and the trip to have enough money to go. I learned a very valuable lesson that day. My mother had given me a plan for the future—benchmarks to help me meet my future goal. I cut grass and shoveled snow that school year, and saved enough money for the trip.

If only I had remembered that lesson after the trip! My journey to financial freedom likely wouldn't have hit so many detours, bumps, and dead ends.

Are you planning for the future or living for the moment? The difference will make or break your life down the road.

Is Your Debt Under Control?

What's the state of your debt? Is it out of control or, if you're fortunate, nonexistent? Mathematically, a strong argument can be made to always maintain some debt. Nonetheless, I believe that mathematics theory and the real world are two very different things. True financial freedom exists when you're no longer bound by the shackles of debt.

> *Stop being a slave to the lender!*

What's Your True Happiness?

As your answers to many of the questions raised in this chapter likely show, happiness is about much more than stuff, and dreams are about much more than instant gratification. That too-expensive fancy car you had to have and that you bought with a second mortgage on your home 10 years ago is long gone, but the payments remain.

Before I had my epiphany, I had to have material possessions that cost me tens of thousands of dollars funded by maxing out my credit cards and becoming enslaved to creditors. That was before I woke up and realized that my true QL wasn't about possessions. As I had briefly realized back at age 18 at that drunken party with fellow high-school dropouts, life is anchored by having purpose. At the time, though, I didn't realize that balance in life, setting goals, and planning for the future were essential components of my happiness.

I offer you the benefit of my hindsight, my experience, my failures and successes over the last two decades with literally thousands of clients, advisors, and more. This is your opportunity to achieve balance and head out on your road to financial freedom. That road starts with the realization of what will make you truly happy.

At age 18, I didn't have an expert financial insider to help me find the right direction, recognize what really matters, and make the best decisions. Instead, I thought I didn't need anyone and could do it on my own. We all know where that led me.

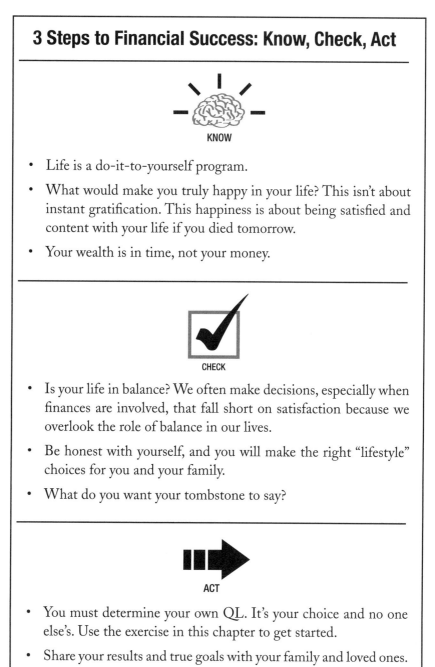

3 Steps to Financial Success: Know, Check, Act

KNOW

- Life is a do-it-to-yourself program.

- What would make you truly happy in your life? This isn't about instant gratification. This happiness is about being satisfied and content with your life if you died tomorrow.

- Your wealth is in time, not your money.

CHECK

- Is your life in balance? We often make decisions, especially when finances are involved, that fall short on satisfaction because we overlook the role of balance in our lives.

- Be honest with yourself, and you will make the right "lifestyle" choices for you and your family.

- What do you want your tombstone to say?

ACT

- You must determine your own QL. It's your choice and no one else's. Use the exercise in this chapter to get started.

- Share your results and true goals with your family and loved ones.

- Put God first in your finances and watch what He does with what's left.

PART II

Your Next Move
The Checks and Balances
Way to Financial Success

"You have a financial choice: Spend now, be sorry later; or save now, be secure later."

— MATT RETTICK

Chapter 5

Duped Into Debt
You Can Get Yourself Out

Your life is My Enterprise, Inc. You are the CEO, the chief executive officer who makes the decisions and determines your future. You're also the CFO—the chief financial officer—who makes the financial decisions.

When a business has more money going out—accounts payable—than money coming in—accounts receivable—generally that company goes belly up. On the other hand, if the company gets expenses and costs under control, the enterprise can thrive.

You have the opportunity today to get control of the costs of your life—My Enterprise, Inc.—and to achieve your Quality of Life Factor (QL). If you act now and are committed to making the right choices—tough though some of them may be—you can achieve your financial freedom.

Waiting for fiscal fitness simply to happen one day doesn't make it so. As you've read, I kept waiting and matters only got worse until I woke up and realized that I had to take responsibility for My Enterprise, Inc., and make my financial freedom happen.

You must wake up to financial reality, take responsibility for your financial present and future, and act now. Only you control your financial future.

The Power of "No"

Your financial freedom begins with learning how to say "No!"—to the sales pitches, to the wants, and to spending beyond your means.

> *"The more 'stuff' you own, the more 'stuff' that really owns you."* —Matt Rettick

Resist Temptation

Salespeople pummel us constantly, pitching their ideas and products—from "fast cash" to "hot deals" and "can't miss" investments. As the CEO and CFO of My Enterprise, Inc., you must see through the clutter. Discerning what's essential and works for your situation is a matter of profit and loss. Your profit and not theirs should be your goal.

> *"We don't really 'own' anything. We only get to 'borrow' it for a short period of time."* —Matt Rettick

Wouldn't it be great if each of us could post "No Solicitation" signs in our windows or doors to keep the pressure to buy at bay? Unfortunately, we can't. You must learn to deal with it, be selective in your choices, and simply say, "No!" to the promotions, "No!" to the marketers, "No!" to the advice-dispensers with products to peddle, and "No!" to the insistent voices inside your head that whisper, "I want it. I need it. I must have it." The bottom line for financial freedom, after all, is freedom from creditors, which gives you the freedom to achieve your QL.

Debt Is *Not* OK

We somehow have been conditioned to believe that debt is a normal part of life. Consumer credit outstanding totaled nearly $2.8 trillion as of November 2012, according to the U.S. Federal Reserve (www.federalreserve.gov/releases/g19/Current/).

Debt absolutely is *not* cool in the New Financial Reality. Crippling debt is *not* a necessary part of living the life of your dreams. It is, instead, a road to financial slavery. Debt should *not* own you; you should control your own life, and the actions you take should help you achieve your goals.

Did you know that even if you have just $5,000 in credit card debt at 13 percent interest, if you pay the minimum $100 each month, you'll end up spending nearly $5,200 in interest and it will take you 21 years to pay off the debt. But if you pay an extra $25 a month, you'll cut the payoff time down to four years, and your total interest expenses drop to $1,590! (source: Vertex42; www.vertex42.com).

As I mentioned earlier, you can make a mathematical case that some level of debt works. Some financial advisors urge people not to pay off their mortgages, even to take out loans on their homes because the interest is deductible, and then use the potential loan payoff money to invest—in their products, of course.

This is all nonsense! The reality of total financial freedom far surpasses mathematics. When we factor in human nature and our buy-more-stuff culture, freedom from the shackles of debt wins easily. You may have all the good intentions in the world to invest or save that extra money, but in the end, it's likely to get frittered away on more stuff rather than put away for a rainy day or spent on a solid investment for the future.

My life is living proof. Before my financial epiphany, there were a number of times—opportunities—when I was ahead financially. But every time I got ahead, I didn't stay ahead. The reason: greed! That's actually the answer to most of our—yours and mine—financial problems. In life, humans want primarily only one thing—more. We want more prestige, more money, more recognition, more sex, more (bigger) houses, boats, cars, and so on. In life, it's called human nature. We become greedy and want more of whatever it is, rather than being satisfied and finding our QL and being content with it.

When I went to Bolivia to build that church, the people's clothes were in tatters and their homes were huts. Yet every morning they were up at 6 a.m., sweeping the dirt off their mud driveways with smiles on their faces. QL is important to these people.

> *"The Bible is often misquoted. It's not money that's the root of all evil. It's the love of money—greed."* —Matt Rettick

Instead of buy, buy, buy and racking up debt and more debt, we must learn to make wise purchases; we must take a Checks and Balances approach—weigh the pros and cons of any purchase before we make it. Always ask yourself whether a prospective purchase is a "want" or a "need," and then make your decision. If you decide to buy, then make sure to get the best possible deal.

Live Within Your Means

Today's headlines are filled with political wrangling in Washington, D.C., over the amount of the federal debt. The United States currently *owes* more than $16.4 trillion and climbing by the second (www.treasurydirect. gov/NP/BPDLogin?application=np).

The government has adopted a spend-now approach that ignores its needs for the future. Trust me, the spend, spend, spend-more mentality eventually catches up with everyone—even the government of the largest country in the Free World. We found that out in 2011 when Standard and Poor's bond rating agency handed the United States its first-ever credit downgrade—from AAA to AA+. Similar to what happens when an individual's credit is downgraded, it then costs more—for the U.S. government, in this case—to borrow money because rating agencies have determined it's at greater risk of default and less likely to pay back loans.

Don't follow the lead of the U.S. government and spend away your future. Instead, try a once-novel approach that today has become a necessity: save, save, save more. You can live within your means, save more for your future, and become financially independent. Just because you could buy a bigger house for no money down, doesn't mean you should!

Even if you feel overwhelmed by financial responsibilities, you must do what it takes now or risk falling victim to the New Financial Reality. Perhaps you owe more money on your home than it's worth, you find yourself supporting your grown kids as well as yourself, or, as happened to me, your credit-card debt threatens to sink you. Whatever the case, you must learn what it takes to start saving now and how to dump your debt, period.

> *You can't borrow your way to financial freedom.*

Conquering the Debt Monster

You already know I do not believe in being a slave to lenders. But let's look at debt another way for a moment.

Too Much Month/Not Enough Money?

Do you end up with too much month at the end of your money? Does your money run out every month before the end of that month? If so, it's time to cut your debt as much as possible. You can't do it overnight. But you can make a difference, and it adds up. Get radical about it. Here are a couple of easy things you can do right away to shrink your debt:

- Sell the stuff you don't need or use—have a garage sale, list it on eBay, or post it on craigslist. Earmark the cash you make to pay off debt. Get rid of anything you haven't used in the past year. That includes golf clubs, boats, jewelry, furniture, and even that vase from your Aunt Sarah. You'll be surprised at how much extra cash you can generate, plus it will de-clutter your space.

- If possible, work overtime or get a second job—even a few hours an evening at a fast-food restaurant works. I realize this is easier said than done. But if you're truly committed to winning your War on Debt!, you must take your financial future seriously. Again, specifically earmark that extra money to go directly toward paying off as much debt as you can.

Forget about debt consolidation as the solution to all your debt problems. That approach simply makes one more creditor rich off your money. In most cases debt consolidation is a cop-out because it doesn't help you kick the habit of accumulating debt. To get out from under your creditors requires a change in your mindset.

When I launched my War on Debt!, I got angry at my debt and targeted it as the enemy. Without regard for which credit card had the highest interest rate, I began to pay off the debts one at a time. I paid off the smallest debt first. We didn't go out to eat; we didn't take vacations (including weekend getaways); we bought generic products; and we bought less food (and wasted less as a result, too). I was able to work more hours and directed the extra cash strictly to pay off our debts. Coupon clipping became a way of life. We tried every generic, off-brand there was because it was less expensive. We shopped at a no-name food warehouse. Some food didn't taste quite as good as the top-of-the-line brands, but it filled our stomachs and kept us going. When I paid off that first debt, I was empowered. I then knew I could do it.

You can do it, too. If your situation doesn't allow you to work more hours, you still can spend less. Forgo the ice cream; buy hamburger instead of steak; eat smaller meals. We ate a lot of soup. And don't tell me times are too tough. Conquering debt isn't easy. But it is an achievable goal.

The Power of Empowerment

During our War on Debt! I might have been a bit hungry occasionally, but I was still alive. I kept at it because I envisioned chains on my ankles and wrists—the chains of debt—just like Jacob Marley's ghost who visited Scrooge in Charles Dickens' *A Christmas Carol.*

As I began to knock off our debts one by one, I became empowered. I then knew that I could control my financial life and achieve the financial freedom I'd always wanted but thought I couldn't have. I was hooked!

Kids Aren't an Excuse

What about the kids? How did they take the cuts and cutbacks? No matter how you think they'll react, the kids will survive. Actually, most children are relatively oblivious to how hard it is for parents to get through tough financial times. Remember my son who had pointed out to me that my Cadillac was missing on that cold February night in Michigan? When that same son was 8 years old, he went with me to buy a very old and very used Ford Maverick for $600. He thought that beat-up old car—not the expensive Cadillac that had been repossessed—was the absolute best car we had ever owned. I had just paid cash for the Maverick and we were puttering down the highway with the windows wide open—the Maverick didn't have air-conditioning. With the wind blowing in his face, my son turned to me and said, "Dad, this car is way better than our other car!"

At the time, I agreed with him. I had paid cash for the car and didn't owe anyone anything on it! I had had a slight—albeit brief—taste of what financial freedom might really be like.

The kids were teens when I launched my War on Debt! That meant they constantly bombarded me with all the usual "gotta haves." But my response was, "No!" That's "no" to the X-boxes, the CDs and DVDs, the clothes-of-the-moment, and more. And guess what? Today the children are in their 30s and early 40s, and they don't even remember what they couldn't or didn't have as teens.

You May Want It, But Do You Really Need It?

Unfortunately, soon after the Maverick moment I reverted to my old spending ways. I got snared again by the hype of consumerism that led to buying things I wanted—and couldn't afford—rather than what I truly needed. I lost track of discretionary spending—all the little extras, and some big ones, too. My spending destroyed us financially. I still had not yet learned the necessity of resisting the temptation to buy things—stuff—I didn't need.

> *The truth is, all we really NEED are the three basics—shelter, clothing, and food/water. Anything more really is to satisfy a want.*

Plastic Power/Weakness. We lived on the third floor of a tacky apartment complex, but I had suits and shirts custom-made. I rationalized that if I looked better, I would sound better and sell more. I had my nails manicured, too, regularly. I had no money, but I did have plastic. I wanted it, so I did it regardless of the fact I couldn't pay for it!

Ever wonder why expressions like, "Act now before it's too late" or "This deal is good for today only" are staples in the world of sales? And why is it that salespeople try so hard to get you to buy something now rather than wait until next week or next month? They know that if you stop to really think about what they're selling, you'll realize you don't truly want it or need it, and you won't buy it.

48-Hour Rule. Next time you're in a buying frame of mind, try the 48-hour rule. When you see something you think you must have, leave it alone and wait 48 hours. If, after that time, you still want to make the purchase, ask yourself, "Do I really need this, or do I simply want it?" If you can live without it, forget the purchase and walk away. You'll discover that you rarely need—or really even want—much of the stuff you have been conditioned to buy. That's the truth even after you achieve financial freedom and affordability isn't a concern.

If, after the 48 hours, you're still determined to make the purchase, pay cash. When it comes to buying anything, plastic—as in credit cards—is the wrong way to go. Your payments are likely to last far longer than your purchases, and you pay many times over for the not-so-cheap thrill of instant gratification. If you can't pay cash for something, you can't afford that something.

Ready, Get Set, Let's Do It

True financial freedom takes more than being able to say "No!" and cutting back. You must lay a solid foundation and develop a serious plan to achieve your QL, and then you'll achieve your happiness for the rest of your life.

Hopefully, by now you've begun to see the shackles from your creditors and decided to get mad at *your* debt. Let's look at the concrete steps you must take to win your War on Debt!

Your War on Debt!

Any successful war needs planning, and that includes a War on Debt! As with any plan, you can't know where you're going or how to get there unless you know your starting point. No one wants to hear the "B" word, as in "budget." But a budget is a necessity in this war. Think of it as simply a word for the cash you have going out and coming in.

> *To get your own customizable, downloadable version of a War on Debt! worksheet, check out the Checks and Balances Financial Success System Workbook online at www.ChecksandBalances.TV.*

The first step in my War on Debt! was to take out a pen and paper. I wrote "War on Debt!" at the top of the page, and then listed all my debts on one side. My list included all the companies and people to whom I owed money, along with how much I owed them—the balance due—and the minimum monthly payment required.

Cash Flow/Your Budget

We all dread budgeting, but in order to win the War on Debt! we also need to understand cash flow—the money coming in and going out. To do that means you must put together a budget. Think of it as a building block to your financial freedom.

Take out two more sheets of paper. At the top of one, write "Outgoing: Fixed Expenses" and list your fixed expenses every month—including the cost of shelter, transportation (including car payments), utilities, and food. Don't forget to include your tax liability on the list. If you're self-employed, especially, it's easy to get trapped into spending money you should be setting aside monthly to cover any federal, state, and local taxes that must be paid either quarterly or annually.

> *To get your own customizable, downloadable version of the Checks and Balances Budget worksheet, check out the Checks and Balances Financial Success System Workbook online at www.ChecksandBalances.TV.*

On the other side of the paper, write "Outgoing: Discretionary" at the top and list what you're spending each month on expenses that are neither fixed nor debt repayment. Those "discretionary expenses" are all the little and big amounts you spend on that stuff—everything from soft drinks and bottled water to Krispy Kremes at the gas station, must-have lipstick, and, yes, all those lattes. (For a little extra incentive, try keeping an expense diary for a month, noting every single discretionary purchase you make. The results likely will shock you—another one of those "aha!" moments.)

Add up both sides of the sheet of paper. Looking at the real numbers of how much you spend is pretty scary. Do you really spend THAT much every month? The answer is, "Yes," and probably more if you weren't brutally honest in your numbers. Let's face it—if you're not being brutally honest, you won't ever achieve true financial freedom.

On your list of expenses—discretionary or fixed—did you include payment to yourself in the form of saving for the future? Most likely, if you're typical, you omitted that expense. If you did include it, kudos! Does it have top priority? Believe it or not, it should (more on that later).

Now at the top of the other blank sheet of paper, write "Incoming: Income." On this sheet list your monthly income—all the money coming in every month from every source. That could mean one paycheck or multiple paychecks plus any alimony, unemployment compensation, dividends, child support, rental income, or whatever might apply to your personal situation. If you're married or living with someone, be sure to include that second paycheck and any other related income.

Now for a real jolt, and not the good kind. Compare the incoming cash with the outgoing cash—the accounts receivable vs. accounts payable for My Enterprise, Inc. As I asked earlier, do you face too much month at the end of your money?

> **MEASURING YOUR DEBT PERCENTAGE**
> *Add up your total monthly income after taxes. Then total your monthly debt payments. Divide your total debt payments into your monthly income. This is the percentage of your after-tax income that funds your debt habit.*

Reality Check/Where to Cut Back

Now you (and your spouse or significant other, if that applies) must figure out where to cut your expenses. Focus on easy ones first, as my wife and I did. I ditched manicures and custom-made suits bought with plastic. We stopped the daily paper. It amounted to a few dollars a week, but every dollar adds up. We stopped going out to dinner. That meant NO meals out. We ate a lot of soup and sandwiches. We shopped at the discount warehouse grocery. We used coupons everywhere we could, and we saved a nickel here, a dollar there, and it added up.

Another great money saver that helped us financially and spiritually: Every Wednesday night, our church had a terrific supper before the church service (many churches do this). For only $5, our entire family ate our fill that evening before the service.

CHECKS AND BALANCES QUICK SAVINGS TIPS

Here are a few to get going:

- Pay off your debt as soon as possible, and don't incur any new debt. It doesn't happen overnight, but if you work hard at it, it will happen. In the interim, make sure you're paying as much as you can on your credit cards each month. Starting now, only pay cash. If you don't have the cash, don't buy whatever it is.

- Take advantage of sales promotions on necessities. Getting a lower interest rate on your car (if you can't pay cash for it) or mortgage may be easier than you think. The only way to know, though, is to explore the options. No matter what marketers say, this is a buyer's market, and that means the ball is in your court. Don't settle for the first interest rate you're quoted. Shop around and compare.

- Take advantage of discounts and coupons: You don't have to be extreme about it, but do look for savings and shop accordingly.

- Cut down monthly expenses. If your cell phone or cable bills seem too high, contact your service provider to find out if they'll lower your bill or change your plan. Often all it takes is a threat to transfer to a competitor to secure a better rate on the spot.

- Take advantage of free or very low-cost meals offered by organizations you're associated with, like churches or other community organizations.

- Don't sabotage yourself with late charges and bounced-check fees, either. That's throwing money out the window and undermines your War on Debt! efforts.

Next, consider your "want versus need" scenarios. Did you really need that new sweater (remember the 48-hour rule)? Could you iron your own shirts with a little spray starch instead of spending $60 a month at the dry cleaners? What about that visit to the dog track? Forget it!

Essential to your War on Debt! is the mantra, "Save now, be secure later." Providing you and your loved ones the financial wherewithal to achieve happiness and security for the rest of your life is paramount. I guarantee that any instant gratification from a fast bet at the dog track, buying that just-released DVD, or purchasing a fancy car will be long forgotten in the context of your life.

Automatic Savings

Don't wait until you've paid all your monthly bills to see if any money is left over to put toward retirement. Pay yourself FIRST! Protect those savings—no matter how small—now. Begin by saving 2 percent of your net weekly or monthly income, then increase it to 5 percent, 10 percent, and eventually 15 percent of your net income. Put the "out of sight, out of mind" philosophy to work for you. The easiest way to save for the future is to have a regular, fixed amount deducted from each paycheck and put into your company's 401(k), a Roth IRA, or other tax-deferred retirement account.

No matter how little or how much our income, each of us must learn to save and invest in our futures. Even if finances are tight, put something away for yourself each and every month. Perhaps start slowly by putting away the money you save from that weekly free or low-cost church meal. That could be an easy way to slip in regular savings. It's an absolute necessity if you don't want to end up an unhappy victim of the New Financial Reality.

Perhaps you know someone like Mike …

Mike lay listening to the soft hum of the machines. Down the hall, he could hear an alarm going off and the pounding of nurses' feet as they ran to help. "How could it all have come to this?" he asked himself. He knew his time was near, and as he reflected on his life, he involuntarily shook his head in disbelief. He closed his eyes and drifted back into a deep sleep.

As a 40-something young man, Mike had lived each day to the fullest. Without thinking of the future, he enjoyed his solid income. Jet

Skis, seasonal trips, dinners out; it was nothing but the best for Mike and his family. He rarely denied himself or his family anything they wanted. In his 50s, with kids in college, money was tight but they got by, although he rarely saved any money. By the time Mike hit his 60s, time for saving had pretty much run out. Then he was laid off, and suddenly the flow of precious cash came to an abrupt stop. Like that, his life turned down a path he could never have imagined.

The stress took its toll on Mike. Arguments and bickering between his wife and him became commonplace. Mike figured he was drinking a bit more than he should, but he consoled himself with the fact that other guys were worse. His kids were grown, spread across the country, and living their own lives. They would send money for a time, but that stopped when the economy took another downward turn.

Eventually Mike and his wife sold their spacious home and moved into an apartment, living off money from the sale. Social Security was their only income. The nice toys, fancy trips, and frequent dinners out were distant memories. These days they lived mostly on pasta and beans. How could his life have come to this?

"Mike! Mike," he heard again. Who was calling his name? Was it a nurse? Mike opened his eyes and became instantly alert. It was Mary, his wife, and she wasn't the old woman he had just imagined. She was still 40-something. Radiant, yet upset, she asked him what was wrong. "Mike," she said, "I think you had a bad dream. Is everything OK?"

Mike sat up and looked around. He wasn't dying in the hospital. He was in his own bed in his own house, and he was his normal 40-something self. "Yes," he said. "A terrible dream." Then suddenly he realized, it hadn't been a dream. It was his wake-up call to the New Financial Reality.

Checks and Balances Tools

Download customizable worksheets and tips at www.ChecksandBalances.TV:

- War on Debt!
- Budget
- Tips to cut back on expenses

Check out weekly financial tips at www.ChecksandBalances.TV:

Download or read our Checks and Balances free reports at www.ChecksandBalances.TV:

- Financial Freedom Wake-up Call
- Financial Freedom Personal Check-up
- The 3 Pillars of the Checks and Balances Life
- The 10 Simple Steps to Financial Freedom

3 Steps to Financial Success: Know, Check, Act

KNOW

- Credit cards do not empower you as a consumer. They enslave you to your creditors.

- The more stuff you own, the more stuff that really owns you.

- As you knock off each debt, you become more empowered.

- Like it or not, a budget is a necessary part of understanding where you are today so that you can plan for where you would like to be down the road.

CHECK

- Live within your means. Write down all your monthly income and expenses. Make future decisions based on what you find.

- Ask your credit-card company or mortgage company how much faster you could pay off your current balance with just one or two extra payments a year.

![ACT arrow icon]

ACT

- Pay yourself first. A regular payment into your retirement account should be a monthly expense just like taxes or utilities or your mortgage.

- Debt is not cool. Commit to your War on Debt! today.

- If you can't pay cash, don't buy it—whatever "it" is (except when it comes to a home or car, if you must).

- Use the 48-hour rule: Wait 48 hours before making a major purchase.

"You must always expect the best, but be prepared for the worst."

— MATT RETTICK

Chapter 6

Expect the Unexpected
Build an Emergency Fund Now!

Financial gain is always a hot topic, but what about its flip side? You rarely hear about financial loss and how to weather life's unexpected financial storms.

Those inevitable storms always seem to hit when we least expect them and are the least prepared. Surviving them shouldn't be an exercise in damage control after the fact.

If you live in a cold climate, when the first big snowstorm hits, people scramble to buy snow tires, snow shovels, and other accoutrements of winter. At the other end of the weather spectrum, if you're in Texas or Florida and a hurricane is headed your way, the mad rush is for bottled water, batteries, and flashlights. Wouldn't it be a wiser approach to recognize that in winter it gets cold and snows, just as in hurricane season hurricanes are possible, and therefore take appropriate steps ahead of time?

Financial storms are no different. You must expect the unexpected and prepare in advance so you can weather whatever happens. With the right moves ahead of time, financial storms often amount to little more than minor glitches.

> *"By failing to prepare, you are preparing to fail."* —Benjamin Franklin

Unfortunately, the vast majority of Americans are ill-prepared for financial storms of any magnitude. That's the finding of the fifth annual Study of the American Dream from MetLife, Inc., a leading global provider of insurance, annuities, and employee benefit programs. The study defines a financial safety net as funds to cover living expenses in the event of illness, job loss, or other serious emergency, and owning financial and protection products like life, home and health insurance, annuities, and retirement accounts. Seventy percent of Americans believe that having a financial safety net is key to achieving the American Dream, yet only 30 percent say theirs is adequate. Among the Baby Boom generation, nearly 75 percent say they lack an adequate safety net.

More than half of those in the study blamed "living paycheck to paycheck" as the reason preventing them from achieving an adequate safety net. A weak retirement savings plan is a close second among Baby Boomers, while younger generations say they are not making enough money to build a financial safety net (www.metlife.com/about/press-room/us-press-releases/index.html?compID=72458).

Why You Must Save

Are you living paycheck to paycheck? If you walked into work tomorrow and your boss handed you a pink slip—whether you were fired or laid off—what would happen to you financially? Could you pay your mortgage? Would you lose your car? Could you feed your family and keep the lights on?

If you never thought you needed to worry about those kinds of things, now is the time to start. In the New Financial Reality, job security—from the assembly line to the C-suite—is a myth. As of December 2012, just over 12 million Americans were out of work—and that doesn't include millions more who have been laid off throughout the recession and have simply given up looking for jobs (www.bls.gov/news.release/empsit.nr0.htm).

Planning Pays Off Even When There Is No Plan!

We've all heard the axiom, "You have to plan your work, and then work your plan." But even the best plans run afoul of distractions and curveballs. You have to be prepared to deal with whatever life throws at you.

By 1999, our kids were grown, and I had reached some degree of sustained financial security. It would be smooth sailing ahead, or so I thought. But life wasn't done sending curveballs my way. That was when I received the middle of the night phone call from my son that propelled us back into the parenting role full-time. Fortunately, by then I had done a good job of socking away cash for unexpected expenses.

I hadn't planned on needing some of that cash to pay legal expenses to gain custody of our grandchildren. But, as I found out that night, there is no "plan." We can't foresee the unexpected that will befall us. But we can prepare to handle the twists and turns that inevitably come our way.

In an ideal world, nothing bad or unexpected would ever happen to us, but you and I know that's not the case—especially in the New Financial Reality. To thrive today, we must be savvy consumers, recognize both sides—the pros and cons, checks and balances—of what's going on around us, and be prepared.

The unexpected has become reality today for far too many Americans. That unexpected could be job loss, disability, or—as happened to me and keeps happening to thousands of other grandparents and parents nationwide—an unexpected increase in financial responsibilities. You can't have financial freedom without enough in savings to pay your basic living expenses for an extended time.

Five years ago, one of my clients—a widow and retiree from Hendersonville, Tennessee—found out firsthand the value of having a financial cushion and being prepared for the unexpected. Long after her husband died and she began drawing on a fixed income, her grown son lost his job. Because of that and medical issues, he had to come back home and look to his mother for financial help. Without her financial cushion, my client, now in her 80s, would not have been able to help her son.

The Definition of "Emergency" Funds

Before you start saving for the future and your retirement, you must save for the unexpected. This isn't cash for a vacation or to buy new furniture or clothes, or even to pay for sudden car repairs. This is money for a real emergency—if you lose your job, if you can't work, or if you or a loved one has a life-threatening health emergency.

What the Statistics Tell Us

Earlier I mentioned some of those major economic indicators we hear discussed regularly. Even if a particular statistic and its movement up or down doesn't directly affect your personal finances at that moment, over time that statistic still may have a cumulative effect on you and your environment. For example, regardless of whether the unemployment rate is up or down any particular month, record levels of Americans are unemployed. Combine that with the climbing rate of inflation, and the result clearly shows a struggling economy. In such an environment, it's doubly important to save for the unexpected.

What if you did lose your job? What are your prospects for getting another one quickly? Of course, that depends in part on you and your skills. But the statistics show a weak U.S. economy that is not creating new jobs—especially well-paying ones—fast enough. Even if you're highly skilled and good at what you do, there's a strong possibility you could be out of work for many months. Clearly, only six months of living expenses socked away in an emergency fund may not be enough today.

A Taste of New Freedom

The New Financial Reality means you'll need to put away perhaps a year's worth of living expenses in the event you're out of work for a long time. That's a tall order, and not everyone can do it. But you'll be amazed at the freedom that comes with knowing you have enough money tucked away to handle an emergency. That kind of freedom translates into personal choices.

Even if you can't afford to save a year's worth of expenses, every extra dollar put into savings helps.

One Step at a Time

Try saving in baby steps. It's the "out of sight, out of mind" approach again. Consistency is a great way to "trick" yourself into saving. If you can't stash big chunks of cash in the bank at once, take a little out of each check and put it away. Make the commitment to save something from every check. Of course, the more you can save, the better, and the quicker you'll reach your goal. As with paying down your debts, when you begin to succeed—in this case, building your emergency fund—you will feel empowered to work even harder to save. I promise that the exhilaration of knowing you're prepared will be worth the hard work.

Proceed With Caution

When it comes to making decisions with financial impact in the New Financial Reality, proceed with caution. If you're self-employed or your employer is struggling or streamlining and may be cutting jobs down the road, now is not the time to refinance a 30-year mortgage down to 15 years unless you have plenty of cash stashed away. Similarly, this is not the time to upgrade to a bigger home. However, if by taking advantage of low interest rates you can lower your monthly mortgage, refinancing is worth considering—especially if you can refinance without having to pay any fees or points. Don't be afraid to negotiate with a lender for that kind of deal. Then, if you have cash left over, make an extra monthly payment earmarked to pay down the principal on your mortgage at the end of the year. It then reduces your overall mortgage more quickly.

Starting Your Emergency Fund

Don't set yourself up to fall short. Saving money is only one side of the savvy-consumer equation. The other is about protecting and preserving your lifestyle, and you can't do that in an emergency if you aren't prepared.

How Much Cash Do You Need?

When figuring how much money to put aside in your emergency fund, remember that it should be enough to cover your essential living expenses for at least six months to a year. That's cash to pay your fixed living expenses—like your mortgage, utilities, transportation, bare-bones food, alimony (or child support) if applicable, and, if you're not debt free, regular monthly payments to keep you on your path to financial freedom.

Discretionary expenses are NOT included and don't figure into the amount of money you should put aside. That means you disregard the cost of new clothes, dinners out, entertainment, and the like.

Your emergency fund is, after all, for emergencies to allow you and your family to hang on temporarily and without losing everything. The goal is to be prepared and help you avoid the traumas like foreclosure that too often befall those who are unprepared.

EMERGENCY FUNDS WORKSHEET

Here is a list of some of the essentials to help you determine your Emergency Fund needs. You'll need to refer back to your War on Debt! and Budget worksheets from the last chapter to pull together the right numbers. Keep in mind that an Emergency Fund is for emergencies, and should not include money for entertainment and other optional expenses.

ESSENTIAL LIVING COSTS FOR ONE MONTH:

Rent/Mortgage:

  Condo/
home association fees:

Utilities:

  Power:

  Water:

  Trash removal:

  Other:

Insurance payments:

  Property:

  Life:

Health:

Disability:

Auto:

Other:

Food:

Medicine (if applicable):

Education (if applicable):

Credit-card and other monthly debt payments (excluding mortgage/rent):

TOTAL:

Now multiply the total by six (as in six months), and that's the minimum amount of money you should put away in a liquid account to have in the event of an emergency.

(For a customizable, downloadable version of this worksheet, visit www.ChecksandBalances.TV.)

Where to Stash Your Cash

Your emergency fund isn't about investing and making money on your money, so it can't be tied up in investments. This is cash socked away in an ordinary bank, credit union, or insured money-market account where it's secure and easily accessible. You leave it alone unless there is a major emergency.

Beware of some money-market accounts that may not be insured. Many unsuspecting consumers, in pursuit of higher interest rates, turned to brokerages to open uninsured money-market accounts. They ended up losing big when the companies ran into financial problems. Read the fine print before you ever sign on the dotted line.

I have maintained $25,000 in emergency cash in a bank account for years. Today, it's earning 0.15 percent, if I'm lucky. I've never really had to use it, but the money is tucked away for a true emergency. I know it's there, and I sleep better at night because of it.

The good news, however, is that you may not have to settle for rock-bottom interest rates on your emergency fund savings account. In today's competitive environment, banks want and need your money, and often offer special, higher interest rates on savings if you just take the time to look for them. Shop around. You might try negotiating for an extra half point or so. Credit unions, which are nonprofits, also may offer competitive rates as well as incentives for bringing in new members. Don't overlook online banks, either. Again, they want your money and often will work to get it.

Thoroughly check out the safety, security, and accessibility of any bank or credit union you're considering before opening an account with them. Any account you open should be FDIC-insured or, in the case of a credit union, insured by the National Credit Union Administration. Both are government agencies that insure accounts up to $250,000. You can check out bank ratings for free in a number of places. Whatever the source, however, make sure the rating group does not accept compensation from the banks and thrifts it rates. Some sources include:

- BankRate.com (www.bankrate.com)
- BauerFinancial.com (www.bauerfinancial.com)

- Federal Reserve Bank
  (www.federalreserve.gov/apps/crape/BankRating.aspx)
- Moody's Investor Services (www.moodys/researchandratings/)
- Weiss Ratings (www.weissratings.com)

If You Have to Use the Cash...

Admittedly, there are times when you think you absolutely have to use your emergency funds. Just because the car—your only transportation—breaks down, though, doesn't mean you have to dip into those funds. Exhaust every other means of solving the problem first. Consider public transportation, car-pooling, or any other temporary option until you can come up with the cash to pay for the repair.

We are talking about your emergency fund—your lifeline if something horrible happens. Think of it in those terms, and you'll be surprised at the other options you can find to pay for that car repair.

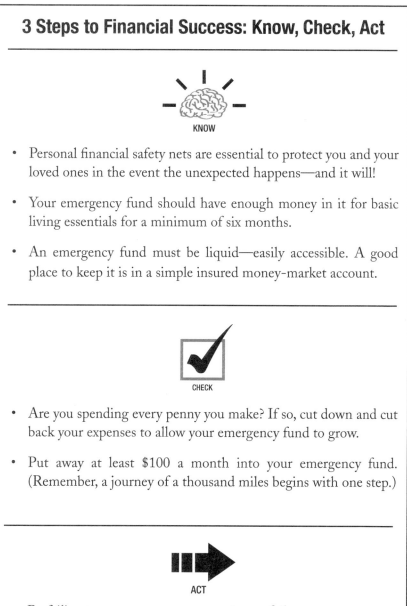

3 Steps to Financial Success: Know, Check, Act

KNOW

- Personal financial safety nets are essential to protect you and your loved ones in the event the unexpected happens—and it will!

- Your emergency fund should have enough money in it for basic living essentials for a minimum of six months.

- An emergency fund must be liquid—easily accessible. A good place to keep it is in a simple insured money-market account.

CHECK

- Are you spending every penny you make? If so, cut down and cut back your expenses to allow your emergency fund to grow.

- Put away at least $100 a month into your emergency fund. (Remember, a journey of a thousand miles begins with one step.)

ACT

- By failing to prepare, you are preparing to fail.

- Be committed to fully funding your emergency fund. Write out your plan of action today!

"Retirement is a marathon, not a sprint."

— MATT RETTICK

Chapter 7

Start Saving for the Future
Retirement or Not, It Takes Money

You can't stop the future, so you best prepare for it—whether your future calls for a planned retirement or whatever else may happen as you grow older.

Each of us should save for the future, and the best time to start is now. Your life and the lives of those you love depend on your planning. The New Financial Reality and the economic uncertainty that accompanies it only add to the urgency.

The smell of the nursing home was sickening—foul and mixed with the stench of impending death. It's been more than 25 years since my grandparents—my father's mother and father— ended up in that Detroit nursing home, but I will never forget its smell.

Grandma Rettick died after about a year there. But my grandfather hung on for 12 long years. I hadn't been close to him—he was tough and crass. Nonetheless, I watched sadly and helplessly as he was stripped of his self-worth, dignity, and money. He became a victim of a system that leaves the unprepared elderly defenseless and at its mercy.

The Facts

None of us sets out to end up hopeless and helpless. My grandparents certainly didn't. I don't want to end up that way, and neither do you. But clearly, unless we put money aside regularly, unless we consistently save now and plan for tomorrow so we can afford to make our own choices, the chances are good that we'll end up running out of cash and at the mercy of charity.

> ### YOUR RETIREMENT IS UP TO YOU
> *When it comes to your retirement, remember that in today's New Financial Reality, it's up to you to ensure you don't outlive your money. You can't count on:*
> - The government to pay your way.
> - Your employer to provide you a dependable, long-term source of income as in a pension.
> - Stock markets to make you rich.
> - The equity in your home to grow and be of use in your retirement.

Before I get into the details of how you can save for retirement, I'd like to share some sobering facts. They're not meant not to scare you, but to jolt you into the reality that you must make the right financial choices now. You have to check the facts, balance them with your needs, and then act accordingly.

Even if you don't think "retirement" is for you, think again. What happens if you get sick or change your mind about retiring? What happens if you get laid off and can't find another job? If you haven't planned and saved ahead of time, you'll likely be out of luck and at the mercy of the system.

Following are some of the statistics:

- If you reach age 65, there's a 40 percent chance you'll have to enter a nursing home at some point (U.S. Department of Health and Human Services, www.medicare.gov/LongTermCare/Static/Home.asp).

- In 2011, the cost of health care nationally reached $2.7 trillion—that's equal to $8,680 per person in the United States (www.cms.gov/NationalHealthExpendData/25_NHE_Fact_sheet.asp).

- The U.S. government expects health-care costs to climb an average 5.7 percent per year through 2021. That's nearly double the average rate of inflation.

- Retirees will need hundreds of thousands of dollars simply to pay for supplemental health-care costs—beyond Medicare coverage. That does NOT include costs for long-term care (www.ebri.org/pdf/briefspdf/EBRI_IB_12-2010_No351_Savings3.pdf).

Delaying Retirement

Age 65 no longer signals immediate retirement, either. In fact, more Americans are postponing retirement for personal and/or financial reasons. Two out of 10 workers say the age at which they plan to retire increased in the last year—36 percent blame the poor economy for their decision (www.ebri.org/pdf/surveys/rcs/2011/FS5_RCS11_Expects_FINAL1.pdf).

The New Age of Aging

Of course, delaying retirement isn't only about economics. The new age of aging is having a profound effect on retirement, too. As we touched on in Chapter 3, Americans are living longer. That means your savings must last longer. Demographics have changed, and marriage is at an all-time low, as well.

Many Baby Boomers have new visions of retirement. Either they don't plan to retire at all or certainly not until they have a specific amount of savings. All this adds to the grim financial future each of us faces if we don't save and plan for tomorrow.

You Can't Count on the System

You can't count on the government to fund your retirement. We know that's not a cynic's view; that's the New Financial Reality. Social Security is in trouble, and so are Medicare and Medicaid. Even if they weren't in trouble, Medicare doesn't cover the cost of assisted living or long-term care (with certain limited exceptions), and Medicaid covers nursing-home care only after your assets are exhausted, with certain restrictions and limitations.

> *"If it's to be, it's up to me'—and it is up to you to put in place an organized approach to putting aside money now for your retirement—however you define it."*—Matt Rettick

Employer pension plans through many companies seem to be going the way of the dinosaur. Many state- and city-funded pensions are in trouble. They're often underfunded, and retirees and soon-to-be retirees face the specter of slashed benefits. In fact, slashing pensions and pension benefits has become the 21st century modus operandi that many companies use to shore up their bleeding balance sheets. As a result, even the U.S. government's Pension Benefit Guarantee Corporation (www.pbgc.gov), established to provide defined-benefit plan protection guarantees for millions of Americans, faces financial problems.

The Importance of a Plan

When it comes to putting aside money for retirement, we don't plan to fail. We fail to plan.

If you're like most people, you probably don't have a formal retirement plan, and that's a big mistake. If your "plan" is "I save as much as I can," that's virtually no plan at all.

I had been very close to my Grandma Wick—my mother's mother. She was a wonderful grandma, who would sit me in a special chair in her kitchen while she whipped up things like blueberry pancakes and biscuits. The aromas that wafted from her creations were so tantalizing. I still remember them, and it's been more than 50 years.

But memories don't pay the bills, and reality can be a stark reminder of the importance of planning ahead. My grandmother developed Alzheimer's disease in 1986. She had no plan and very little money saved for the unexpected. She hadn't planned to get sick. One day everything was rosy, and the next the walls caved in. What little savings she had were quickly devoured by the cost of her care. Luckily, my Aunt Lorna, my mother's sister, was able to take care of her. But it certainly wasn't an easy six years that my aunt spent as a full-time caregiver. It would have been catastrophic for my grandmother if my aunt had not been there to help her.

Details Count

A real plan has a defined outcome—living your QL, for example—with a deadline in place. For example, if you plan to go to the movies and don't look at the schedule, you have an "idea" and not a plan. Whereas if you had said, "I plan to go to the 7:15 p.m. showing of the new Tom Hanks movie at the Acme MegaPlex," that's a plan.

So what's your plan for retirement? Your answer should be as detailed as the following: "I plan to retire at age 62 with about 50 percent of my current income and live debt free. With Social Security—if it's still around—I should have about 75 percent of my working income."

Put your plan in writing. A plan that's not in writing is not a plan.

Components of Your Plan

In a perfect world—if you do everything right—the pattern for your financial savings should translate into the Four Seasons of Your Financial Life:

- **Accumulation.** Generally through around age 55 (or when your children, if you have them, are grown), you lay the foundation for your financial life with savings, tax-saving strategies, and structuring your retirement plan.

- **Preservation.** Usually age 55 to retirement—your goal shifts to protecting your life savings and cutting your investment risks while still trying to earn better-than-average returns.

- **Distribution.** The period when your savings are structured to provide you and your spouse or significant other income to last throughout your retirement years.

- **Succession.** If you've done all the right planning, after your death your remaining life savings are passed to your loved ones in a tax-efficient manner.

Of course, this isn't a perfect world. With today's New Financial Reality, each of us must deal with different financial responsibilities at different ages and stages of our lives. That doesn't mean, though, that you can't use the above as a guide and then work to achieve the goals of each stage in your own time frame.

Be Realistic

Is your plan a realistic one considering your income? It should be. From the time I was 18 until well into my 40s, I approached business with the idea to get rich quick. Although there's nothing wrong with lofty goals, there's no use planning a pipe dream. I learned that the hard way.

We talked about goals and your QL in Chapter 4. Make sure any plan you lay out to achieve those goals is realistic and attainable. Otherwise, you'll become quickly disillusioned, lose focus, and end up as I did so many times—a victim of the vicious boom/bust financial cycle.

Instead, lay out a workable plan that takes baby steps toward your goal. That's how I reached my financial freedom. We paid off one credit card bill at a time, and we grew more empowered to reach our major goal with every debt marked "Paid in Full."

Don't allow snags in your plans to derail you, either. The key is to be flexible and to keep working toward your goal. When I was in what should have been the Preservation of my savings stage, I suddenly found myself facing the cost of braces for my grandchildren, along with all the other expenses of parenting. It was tough, but I kept sight of my goal and didn't lose focus. We continued to cut unnecessary expenses and worked to limit our taxes and the fees in our portfolio. It may have taken us a bit longer to achieve our goal, but we did it one baby step at a time.

Work Your Plan

A plan is successful only if you pay attention to it. Revisit your plan regularly—not every few years, but at least once EVERY QUARTER. Review the plan with a critical eye: Are you on track? If not, why not? What, if anything, is missing? What can you do to get back on track? Are you ahead of schedule? If so, don't slack off; press on.

No plan is perfect. Even the best plan is only a good plan that will need to be monitored and modified to take into account life's inevitable twists and turns. Also, don't overlook the fact that your QL can change. If it does, change your plan to accommodate the needs of your new QL.

The "Pocket" Approach to Saving

An easy way to make sure you're putting money away for all the right things—including your retirement—is to think of your savings as various "pockets" of money. Each pocket is for a specific use, and its contents can be invested or placed in different types of savings vehicles with various levels of risk depending on the pocket's purpose. (For more on various approaches to saving, visit www.ChecksandBalances.TV and check out the Checks and Balances Financial Success System Workbook.)

Pockets and Their Purpose

Your car pocket, for example, is where you regularly save money to buy your next car. Remember, with the War on Debt! you should pay cash for everything. Your clothes pocket is where you put aside money for clothes—not the frivolous kind, but the necessities. A simple FDIC- or FCUA-insured money-market account makes sense here—your money earns a small amount and still is readily accessible. The education pocket holds savings for perhaps your children's or grandchildren's college. A tax-advantaged 529 savings plan is the best place for the contents of that pocket. Your retirement fund is yet another pocket, and one that takes precedence over all the other pockets *except* your emergency fund. It's that pay-yourself-first approach again.

Funding the Pockets

You must adopt a formal approach to filling the various pockets with cash. Again, the best intentions mean nothing without a formal plan. Remember, 2 percent of something is better than 100 percent of nothing in the future!

A certain amount from every paycheck needs to be put into each pocket. Depending on how you're paid, you'll be funding your pockets monthly, bimonthly, weekly—perhaps even seasonally. But whenever and however you're paid, money must go into your various pockets. How much? That depends on how much you earn and how many fixed costs and obligations you have. You must be realistic as well as consistent when filling your pockets.

HOW MUCH TO SAVE

When I started saving in earnest, I would sit down with my three sons every Sunday after church and teach them how money works. The lessons I taught them about how much to spend and save hold true today for all of us.

I only get to spend 45 cents (45 percent) of every dollar I earn.

The remaining 55 cents (55 percent of that dollar) are used to pay for nondiscretionary items that include:

- 10 cents (10 percent) I tithe to my church.
- 30 cents (30 percent) goes to Uncle Sam for taxes.
- 10 cents (10 percent) goes into my emergency fund until it's fully funded.
- 5 cents (5 percent) goes to my retirement accounts.
- After my emergency fund is fully funded, I put 15 cents (15 percent) in my retirement accounts.

Breaking down the remaining 45 cents:

- Discretionary savings and expenses
- Food
- Housing
- Utilities
- Car savings
- Clothing
- Entertainment
- Insurance
- Extras

As your financial situation changes, so do the amounts allotted to each pocket. For instance, when you've won the car battle in your War on Debt! and have paid off your car loan, the amount you formerly sent to the auto lender every month can now be reallocated. You could put the entire amount into your auto pocket against the day when you need a new car. Or, you could put some of the money into the auto pocket and some into the pocket of a more pressing debt. (If you haven't paid off your car loan and are unable to sell the car to pay cash for a less expensive one, don't despair. Remember, it's about baby steps. As long as you consistently put something—no matter how small—into each pocket, you will come out ahead.)

RETIREMENT SAVINGS TIP

If you rely on automatic direct deposit for your regular paycheck, ask your employer to split the deposit into two deposits. If you can afford it, ask for 10 percent to 15 percent to be deposited into your 401(k) or other pension plan and the rest into your savings or checking account. Watch your retirement savings grow.

Your Retirement Pocket

The amount of money you will need for a comfortable retirement depends on your QL. You must determine what it is that will bring you happiness in your later years. Don't buy into all you hear about retirement costing less, either. Retirement—even the bare-bones variety—costs money and plenty of it. As I mentioned earlier, health-care costs alone can reach into the hundreds of thousands of dollars without factoring in inflation!

Worse still, the New Financial Reality adds to the problem. Tumbling housing prices combined with market losses spell retirement cash shortfalls for many Baby Boomers. Still others who thought they did everything right for retirement will come up cash short because they didn't save enough and with guarantees of their principal in mind.

Dollars and Cents

There are many approaches to figuring the actual dollar amount you'll need in retirement. That's why working with a true financial advisor and taking the Checks and Balances approach is so important. When I work with clients, we start by considering what amount of money they want or need by the time they're 60, 70, 80, and so on, and then we work backwards from there.

WHAT IT TAKES

The following charts illustrate the approximate amount of monthly savings required to create a specific monthly income in retirement (does not reflect taxes or inflation)*:

3 Percent Annual Return

Starting Age	$1,000/month at age 65	$2,000/month at age 65
25	$ 183	$ 365
30	$ 228	$ 456
35	$ 290	$ 580
40	$ 379	$ 758
45	$ 515	$1,030
50	$ 745	$1,489
55	$1,210	$2,418
60	$2,620	$5,230

6 Percent Annual Return

Starting Age	$1,000/month at age 65	$2,000/month at age 65
25	$ 85	$ 170
30	$ 119	$ 237
35	$ 168	$ 336
40	$ 244	$ 487
45	$ 365	$ 730
50	$ 580	$1,160
55	$1,030	$2,060
60	$2,416	$4,830

Assuming interest is paid monthly on the account value.

Just Do It

To build a foundation, you must start somewhere. It takes sacrifice. But just as you can win your War on Debt!, you also can accomplish retirement security.

When I began saving money for my retirement, I could afford to put aside only $200 a month. If your War on Debt! is an especially fierce one, you might be able to afford only $50 a month. That's OK. You can work your way up from there. Eventually I worked my way up to saving $1,000 a month in my retirement pocket. I haven't quit yet, and neither should you. Keep saving money regularly in your retirement pocket even after you retire.

Think of your savings as I do, in terms of delayed gratification—what you'll want and need tomorrow instead of what you think you want today. When you're 65, 75, or 85, you'll be grateful for every penny you saved.

Keep in mind, too, that the more time your money has to compound, the less you need to save to meet your needs for the future. If your goal is to have $1 million saved for retirement by age 65 and you're age 50 today, you'll need to put aside $4,400 a month to achieve your goal, assuming average earnings of 3 percent ($3,450 a month at 6 percent average earnings). On the other hand, if you start saving at age 25, it takes only $1,080 a month, assuming the same 3 percent average earnings, to reach your goal ($500 a month with average earnings of 6 percent).

Where to Put Your Retirement Savings

With the New Financial Reality, it's not enough simply to save money. You must make the right moves with your money as you save. The right investment/savings strategy factors in your QL—and what it will take to maintain it—as well as inflation, market volatility, and more.

To 401(k) or Not

If your company or employer offers a 401(k) or 403(b) plan, take advantage of it. These plans—named for the section of the Internal Revenue Service code that created them—are great, with a few caveats in light of the New Financial Reality. The responsibility to fund these retirement vehicles is solely up to the individual employee. Even if your employer offers some type of matching funding, it's your responsibility to figure out how much to save and where to invest the money. Too many Americans have opted not to save enough or, in the past several years, have lost life savings in 401(k) plans invested solely in their company's stock. When the companies failed, the savings in their 401(k) plans vanished. Two notorious examples are Enron and WorldCom.

Another big problem is that some account holders have used and still use the accounts as safety nets rather than for their intended purpose—retirement. They use the money to pay down medical bills, to make down payments on homes, or for extra cash when a spouse loses a job. Then the markets plummeted—think of the Great Recession of 2008–2009. The bottom line today is that many people now are staring retirement in the face with little or no retirement savings.

> *In a recent Checks and Balances TV online poll, 28 percent of the respondents said they planned to rely the most on their 401(k) plan to fund their retirement. I hope those people have other retirement savings because banking your retirement strictly on the whims of the stock market can be a risky proposition.*

A word of warning with 401(k) plans: Do NOT allocate all your retirement funds in the stock market, or you could end up like so many would-be retirees who can't afford to retire because their nest egg fell by 30 percent to 50 percent just as they were about to retire.

No 401(k)? You Have Other Options

Despite the recent recession and subsequent trillions of dollars of investment losses by so many people, alternative income sources for retirement are, fortunately, available. These options allow you to build your own retirement security as opposed to relying solely on the government, including Social Security.

As we discussed earlier, not everyone has the option of an employer-sponsored pension plan. If that's the case, keep in mind that the IRS has tax-advantaged limits on many of the plans in the alphabet soup of retirement options. The rules can address tax deductibility, contributions, withdrawals, and income qualifications. A few retirement options include:

- **Traditional IRAs.** Tax-advantaged retirement savings vehicle; ability to contribute pre-tax dollars is not limited by income thresholds, but tax deductibility is; earnings grow tax-deferred; taxes due when you begin withdrawing money from the account; mandatory withdrawals after age 70½ (withdrawal penalties prior to age 59½).

- **Roth IRAs.** Income threshold to qualify for a Roth IRA; funded with after-tax dollars, but qualified withdrawals can be tax free; no mandatory withdrawals at any age (withdrawal penalties prior to age 59½).

- **SEP (Simplified Employee Pension).** Tax-advantaged individual retirement account in which your employer or you as a self-employed person can contribute up to the lesser of $50,000 or 25 percent of your annual compensation; no tax on your initial contributions; taxes are due in the year of withdrawals; mandatory withdrawals after age 70½ (withdrawal penalties prior to age 59½).

- **SIMPLE (Savings Incentive Match Plan for Employees**). Tax-advantaged retirement option for employees of small employers (100 or fewer employees); includes employee salary reductions and matching contributions; generally self-administered; taxes are due on withdrawal; mandatory withdrawals after age 70½ (withdrawal penalties prior to age 59½).

For more information on these and other types of retirement plans and their tax ramifications, check out the Internal Revenue Service's free brochures online (www.irs.gov/retirement/index.html).

The best approach to retirement savings with these plans is to invest the maximum allowed by law each year, and then look to other investment options that will maximize your long-term security, create regular income streams, and minimize your taxes and fees. We'll talk about some of the options with your longevity in mind in Chapter 11.

Make Sure Your Nest Egg Is Invested Properly

Investing your nest egg properly will help you make the most of what you've saved. The key is to align your portfolio with your current retirement goals—to ensure your QL. That means you make the right financial choices now—invest in the proper savings vehicles—so you can afford to do what you like later.

Inflation should be factored into the equation, too, and I don't mean a simple 3 percent increase in the cost of living. (Historically, inflation is about 3 percent per year.) Consider that since 1950, the cost of living has risen nearly 800 percent. When many of us were born, a gallon of gasoline cost 27 cents. A first-class stamp was only 3 cents, and a loaf of bread, 14 cents. Today, gas flirts with $4 to $5 a gallon; a stamp is 46 cents and climbing, and bread easily costs $3 a loaf.

THE INVISIBLE CULPRIT—INFLATION

Based on a 3 percent annual inflation rate, see what happens to your money's buying power over time:

Today: $10,000

After 10 years: $7,441

After 20 years: $5,537

After 30 years: $4,120

Source: "Growth Without Risk," Matthew J. Rettick, 2011

Don't count on the "average rate of return" when it comes to selecting the right investment, either. Often these averages are based on unrealistically long periods of time, especially when it comes to the stock market.

Wall Street has failed the American people. So says my colleague Ron Roberts, a financial professional and retirement planning expert in Jackson, California (Roberts Retirement Group, www.robertsretirement.com). He likens investing in stocks—Wall Street—to gambling in a Las Vegas casino. "You want to win big and in a very few cases some may, but 'the house' always wins…(while) the common Joes of America lose."

With the great market crash in the early part of the 20th century—1929–1932—the Dow dropped 89 percent. It took investors 25 years to recover—just to get their money back from their losses without earning anything additional. When the markets go down, what happens to people who are 50, 60, 70 years old? How many years do they have left to rebuild? If the market drops, how many years will you have left to rebuild?

MARKET ROLLER COASTER
Will you live long enough to recoup your losses in the stock market?

- Suppose you invested $100,000 on March 10, 2000, the day the Nasdaq hit its all-time high of 5,132.

- By October 10, 2002, the Nasdaq had dropped to 1,108, and your investment was worth $21,590—a loss of more than 78 percent.

- To recoup the loss of your principal would require 463 percent growth.

- Assuming an 8 percent annual return, it would take 20 years to recoup your loss.

Keep in mind that retirement is not a single point in time. Depending on your longevity, it's possible that you may be retired longer than you were employed. When planning for retirement, you must factor in cost increases for basic needs—and that's not including health-care cost increases.

Diversification

As many 401(k) account owners at Enron and WorldCom discovered, lack of diversification can be the death knell for your retirement savings. Never put all your eggs in one basket—stocks or bonds. That doesn't mean own as many different stocks in as many different companies as possible. It means you dilute or spread out your money across multiple investments and companies. Then, if one crashes, you've minimized your losses.

In investment management jargon, spreading the risk by putting your money in different types of investments with varying risks is known as asset allocation. For a minute, let's forget about investing and consider what would happen to your corner grocery if it carried only one product or one brand. That likely wouldn't be too good for its business or its bottom line. The same is true for your retirement savings. It takes the right group of investments with varying volatility to protect your nest egg. It's up to you as a savvy investor, along with the knowledge of your true financial advisor, to determine the mix of investments that works best for your retirement savings plan.

The Risk Factor

To figure the right degree of risk in retirement investing, I use the "Investment Rule of 100," with a few nuances factored in. The basic strategy: Subtract your current age from 100, which stands for the age you potentially could live to, and invest the remainder, expressed as a percentage, in higher-risk accounts. For example, if you're 40 years old, subtract that number from 100, which leaves a remainder of 60. That means 60 percent of your retirement savings should be invested in somewhat volatile accounts. The remaining 40 percent should be invested in guaranteed or safe accounts.

Basically, investments are divided into three risk categories:

- **High risk.** Small- and mid-cap stocks; small- and mid-cap stock funds; and alternative investments like options, futures, currency, gold, silver, and real estate.

- **Moderate risk.** Large-cap stocks and stock funds; bonds; bond mutual funds; preferred stocks; REITS (real estate investment trusts); ETFs (exchange-traded funds); and variable annuities.

- **Low risk.** Fixed annuities; declared-rate annuities; fixed indexed annuities; certificates of deposit; U.S. Treasury bills, bonds, and notes; savings accounts; money-market accounts, and U.S. savings bonds.

Again, you should invest your money depending on your financial needs and risk level at any period in your life. Different people are comfortable with different levels of risk. (To assess your comfort zone when it comes to risk, take our Checks and Balances Risk Assessment Quiz online at www.ChecksandBalances.TV.)

COMPONENTS OF YOUR RISK TOLERANCE

Investment decisions are a trade-off between risk and return.

- Risk: Any possibility of loss to your portfolio value.

- Return: Amount earned or profit on an investment.

Generally, investments with the highest potential for gains carry the greatest risk of loss.

Your personal risk tolerance level depends on a variety of factors, including your investment objectives, toleration for losses, investment performance expectations, and more. Above all, however, you must be comfortable with the level of risk in your portfolio.

If someone pitches you an investment in stocks, bonds, or mutual funds as the best long-term investment, take the Checks and Balances approach. Think twice and weigh the pros and cons of each investment. As long-term, low-risk safe havens for your hard-earned cash, many investments simply don't fill the bill. Your nest egg should be invested for maximum return with minimal risk and limit your taxes and fees in the process.

Stocks, bonds, and mutual funds may be suitable investments for a portion of your cash after you've invested your nest egg with the security of your principal foremost in mind.

At the opposite end of the spectrum, investing in nothing but ultra-conservative financial vehicles can erode your nest egg over time. If, for example, your money is safe from stock market loss but the interest you're earning after taxes doesn't keep pace with inflation, you're losing buying power. To protect your nest egg, regularly re-evaluate your investments (tweak your plan!) and make any necessary changes to help hedge against inflation.

Checks and Balances Tools

Download or read our free reports at www.ChecksandBalances.TV:

- The Truth About Retirement
- The Truth About Social Security
- The Truth About Retirement
- The Truth About How to Become a 21st Century Investor

Take the CBTV Risk Assessment Quiz online at www.Checksand Balanaces.TV.

Download our free checklists at www.ChecksandBalances.TV to use before buying any major purchase or investment.

- Stocks
- Mutual funds
- Bonds

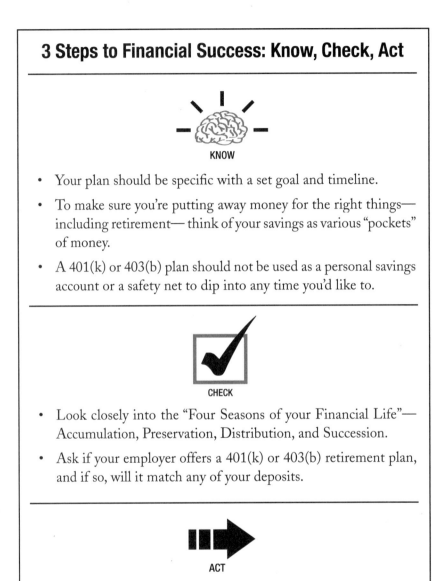

3 Steps to Financial Success: Know, Check, Act

KNOW

- Your plan should be specific with a set goal and timeline.

- To make sure you're putting away money for the right things—including retirement— think of your savings as various "pockets" of money.

- A 401(k) or 403(b) plan should not be used as a personal savings account or a safety net to dip into any time you'd like to.

CHECK

- Look closely into the "Four Seasons of your Financial Life"—Accumulation, Preservation, Distribution, and Succession.

- Ask if your employer offers a 401(k) or 403(b) retirement plan, and if so, will it match any of your deposits.

ACT

- "If it's to be, it's up to me"—and it's up to YOU to put money aside every week/month for your future.

- Begin putting away 1 percent or 2 percent of your net income for retirement—2 percent of something is better than 100 percent of nothing in the future.

- Apply the "Investment Rule of 100" to your investment strategy.

"You have to go out on a limb if you ever expect to get the fruit."

— MATT RETTICK

Chapter 8

Become a Savvy Consumer
Negotiate Every Purchase You Make

Unlike elsewhere in the world, few Americans are accustomed to bargaining with sellers to lower the prices of their products. We negotiate the prices of major purchases like real estate and cars, but little else. Negotiating the price of a handbag in a trendy boutique or a dishwasher at the hardware store is as foreign to us as "haggling" over a carpet at a Turkish bazaar.

If we want to pay a lower price, generally we wait until the item is on sale or we can get a special "coupon" or discount. In the New Financial Reality, however, that attitude must change.

Get ready to negotiate for the best price on goods and services. That goes not only for the house or new car, but for your child's braces (yes, professionals willingly make deals), clothes at the chain department store, and home repairs. Negotiating doesn't mean being "cheap." It means you're a savvy consumer who pays the lowest price in an unstable economy.

In today's highly competitive marketplace, nearly everyone will make a deal. All you have to do is ask. If someone does say "no," you can always pay the higher price or say "Thank you very much" and go across the street to find a better deal. The much more likely scenario, however, is that you'll be amazed by how quickly the seller is willing to work with you, the buyer, for your business.

107

The New Reality

For many of us, the idea of negotiating has negative overtones. For some, it conjures the image of haggling over a loaf of bread because we don't have the money to pay for it. (As a kid, I had to negotiate because we really couldn't afford necessities.) Others think of negotiating as the nerve-racking process of fighting with a used-car dealer to keep from being ripped off. We've all done that!

Neither scenario, though, fits the profile of negotiating the best price in the New Financial Reality. I'm talking about negotiating your way to huge savings in a marketplace where thousands of professionals and businesspeople *expect* you to want to get the best possible price. My son Jeremy even has an app on his iPhone that allows him to scan a bar code on an item in any store, and then it provides prices for the item on the Internet.

Remember, you have what every business wants—your money. Nearly every business or professional fights direct competition for your dollars and their survival. For the consumer, that's the ticket to taking control of the sales process. Unless they're the only game in town—and how often is that the case, especially when you factor in the Internet—the business or professional needs you more than you need them. You can always take your business elsewhere. You know it, and they know it.

Many businesses offer to beat their competitors' prices. That's why I make it a point in the negotiating process to let contractors and professionals know upfront that I'm getting several estimates or second opinions. Just because the plumber, electrician, or doctor says something will cost a certain amount doesn't mean that's the price you have to pay.

> *"I cannot afford the luxury of allowing my emotions to control my attitude and my actions."* —Matt Rettick

Be brave, and ask for a better price. Be fair, though. And, as Jeremy says, "You do *not* get what you do not ask for!" You'll definitely like the results—extra savings for you.

When You Least Expect It

I negotiate for everything. I don't haggle, but I do discuss, and I'm not afraid to ask for the best price. Nonetheless, until recently it had never occurred to me to negotiate with medical professionals for their services until two of my grandsons needed braces.

I wanted our grandsons to go to the top orthodontist in our area—I'll call him Dr. O. I knew the braces were likely to cost $10,000 or more—a big cash outlay by any standards. Jeremy recently had told me how much money he had saved on braces for himself, his wife, Nomi, and their daughter, so I thought I would try it myself.

I did my homework. I called two other orthodontists in the area to inquire about the price of braces for my two grandchildren. Armed with the knowledge of his competitors' pricing, we went to visit Dr. O's office. I told him we wanted the best for our grandsons, but that his prices were on the high side. I also said, "I have spoken to a number of your competitors, and they have offered me the same service for less."

Professionals—Dr. O included—are businesspeople who survive only if they have enough business. If they're not willing to negotiate, they will lose business—yours included—to their competition. We ended up saving $4,000 on our grandsons' braces, and all because I took the time to check with the competition and then ask for a better price.

Of course, I knew Dr. O would do the best job, and I wanted to hire him. But I didn't let him know that. To negotiate successfully, I needed to let Dr. O know that I would walk away to his competitor if he didn't give me a better price. He did, and I saved plenty.

Even Chain Stores Deal

Today is a buyer's market. Any item you need probably is widely available—including online—and often with widely varying prices. Recognize that and don't be afraid to deal. Salespeople and professionals won't look at you with disdain simply because you ask for a better price. Even if you can afford the higher price, it makes no sense to pay it if you don't have to. This is about being a savvy consumer.

I was in a large department store recently and saw a shirt I liked but thought it was too expensive. I actually had seen the same or similar shirt for less in another store. When I mentioned that to the sales clerk, she immediately offered to give me a discounted price, no questions asked. It can be that simple. Ask the question, "Is that your best price?"

More Savings

The master negotiator Jeremy told me that when he's purchasing ANYTHING that costs more than a couple hundred dollars, he always asks for a minimum of a 10 percent discount to see what the salesperson says.

Don't hesitate to let a seller know upfront that you're paying cash, too. Jeremy automatically saves 2 percent to 4 percent on his purchases simply by paying cash, and that's without even starting the negotiating process.

You Can Do This

Get ready to deal. When making big purchases—including cars—keep in mind that the best time to buy is at the end of the month, quarter, or year because salesmen and companies must meet sales quotas and generally will bend over backward to do so.

In 1996, I finally had triumphed in my War on Debt! I had paid off all our debts—the smallest to largest—except the mortgage, which was down to about $100,000. I had saved enough money to drive newer cars, and I decided I had earned the privilege of driving the car I'd always wanted—a Lexus. I considered it my personal symbol of financial success and thought it would fit my ego and make me feel good about myself—as long as I paid cash for it!

I went to the Lexus dealership near our home in Madison, Tennessee, at the end of September. As a savvy consumer, I didn't ask to see the new cars. (Never buy a new car; always look for one with low mileage that's a year or two old, and you'll save thousands of dollars.) I asked the dealer to see his newer used cars. The dealer showed me a beautiful tan one-year-old Lexus LS400 with leather interior and 18,000 miles on it. I sat in that '95 Lexus and immediately was smitten. I wanted this car. I took it for a test drive, and I knew this was the car of my dreams—the feel of it, the smell of the leather, and all the extras were exactly what I wanted. BUT, I couldn't show that this was the car for me. In order to successfully negotiate with the dealer—as in any negotiation—I had to convey instead that I could live without this purchase.

So I said to the salesman, "The car looks nice and feels good. How much do you want for it?" He quoted me a $50,000 price tag, nowhere near the amount I intended to pay for the car. I had done my homework and knew the pricing of similar cars. I also knew that when it comes to cars, the first and second offer is NEVER the dealer's best offer. The secret to successful negotiations, though, is to know that the seller has to make money, too.

He then asked what I was willing to pay for the car. I offered him $40,000—significantly less than I was willing to pay. I knew he couldn't accept that amount, but I offered it so he would say, "There's no way we can do that."

The negotiations "game" had begun. You can't negotiate seriously without the back and forth of a Ping-Pong game. You have to be willing to walk away, too, and I was.

With the Lexus, the game took 45 minutes—mostly because the salesman had to go back and forth to his boss for approval (or at least pretend he did). The end result was that I saved $7,000, and it all happened while I was in the showroom.

We settled on the $43,000 price, and to the salesman's amazement, I told him I was paying cash. He did his best to try to get me to finance the car and even said, "Invest the cash in the stock market instead!"

I responded, "Joe, apparently you've never been debt free before, have you?" He said, "No, I haven't. Why?" I smiled and told him he probably wouldn't understand. Then I paid cash for my new car and proudly drove it away. It has been more than 15 years and several cars later, and I still enjoy the elation of paying cash and driving away with no big debt hanging over my head every month.

Checks and Balances Approach to Successful Negotiation

You have the ability and the right to negotiate. Believe in yourself, and you will be able to negotiate successfully on nearly all the goods and services you need or want. Do so, though, with your budget in mind. Pay cash if you can, and enjoy your financial freedom.

Every time you spend a dollar, say:

"Mr. Seller, I'm interested in your (product or service), but I want the best value for my money. What's the best price you can offer me today if I pay cash?"

At this point in the discussion, it doesn't matter whether you actually plan to pay cash. You're simply trying to start the negotiations and discover the seller's first offer. Remember, it's not the final offer, either. (If you do actually end up financing your purchase, the seller is always happy to accommodate you because he or she makes more money on the purchase.)

Never appear satisfied or pleased with the first reduced-price offer. If you've done your homework, you should know whether the offer is a fair one. Counter the offer with a few words related to the competition. For example, when negotiating the price for our grandsons' braces, I pointed out to Dr. O that his competitors offered the same work for several thousand dollars less. If you're buying a car, try something like: "Really? That's only X dollars off list price."

Then be silent. Don't talk! You've laid your cards on the table. You've pointed out the stated price is too high, and you aren't willing to pay it. You've shown the seller you've done your homework and know the list price of a similar product. Let the seller think about what you've said. Eventually, he or she likely will say something such as, "What did you have in mind?" or, "What price will it take to earn your business today?"

The ball is back in your court. Return it with gusto: "You've been very helpful today, and I would like to do business with you. But unless I can purchase this item for (20 percent to 40 percent off the retail price), then I'm going to have to go to (name one or two competitors) and see what they can offer me."

You Can Always Walk Away

I promise you that the salesperson, manager, or owner of the business will try very hard to earn your business that day by making a counteroffer that's between your offer and his or her previous offer. Keep in mind that the seller has to make money in the deal. But if you're not satisfied with the offer, then walk out! Yes, you can find what you want elsewhere. When I bought that first Lexus, I really wanted *that* car. But if the dealer hadn't lowered his price, I would have walked out.

You may be surprised, too. I've had salespeople and professionals rethink their original decision, and work even harder to get my business after I've left their premises. The bottom line is that you'll end up the proud owner of the item you wanted—along with extra cash in your pocket.

Homework Pays Off

Sometimes, simply by doing your homework, you can end up with great savings. Jeremy has done that many times, especially when it comes to buying electronics. In one instance, he wanted a stereo receiver to go with his new Bose surround-sound speakers. After looking at various products and prices online, he decided on a Yamaha model that retailed for $450.

Armed with his research, Jeremy walked into a local big-box electronics store, asked for the manager of electronics, and told him he wanted to purchase the receiver from a local store, but he could get a better price online. The manager asked Jeremy the online price. Jeremy told him it was $400 including shipping, with no tax since the online company was not in Tennessee (our state sales tax is up to 9.75 percent). The manager told Jeremy to follow him. They walked to a workstation where the manager pulled out a calculator, punched in a few numbers, then offered Jeremy the receiver he wanted for $365.

The two then walked to the checkout stand, made the deal, and Jeremy walked out with his receiver—no bartering, no haggling, no involved discussions. Saving money can be that easy!

NEGOTIATING ESSENTIALS

- Don't be afraid to deal.
- Be fair. The goal, after all, is for both you and the seller to be happy with the outcome.
- Do your homework. Know what competitors charge for the same goods and services.
- Silence is golden. Once you've laid your cards on the table, don't talk. The next person who does likely will be the loser.
- Be willing to turn around and walk away if the deal isn't right.

Beyond Cash: Be Creative

Be creative in your negotiations. Some vendors may be willing to barter—to trade goods and services for your services instead of cash. You won't know if you don't ask. Years ago I traded my sales training services for a new $1,200 Kirby vacuum sweeper. I also negotiated all the frozen food—meats and vegetables—for our family for five years plus a new fancy freezer in exchange for providing sales training to a food company's direct-marketing firm. They had what I wanted—food and equipment; I had what they wanted—sales training skills—so we negotiated a deal that made both of us happy.

If you do end up bartering your services in exchange for goods or services, don't forget to claim whatever you receive in trade as income on your taxes.

Checks and Balances Tools

Download or read our free report at www.ChecksandBalances.TV:

- Negotiating Your Way to Huge Savings

Download our free checklists at www.ChecksandBalances.TV to use before making any major purchase or investment:

- New or used automobile
- New or pre-owned home
- Repairs on your home or car
- Furniture
- New or used boat
- Appliances
- Home entertainment
- And much more

3 Steps to Financial Success: Know, Check, Act

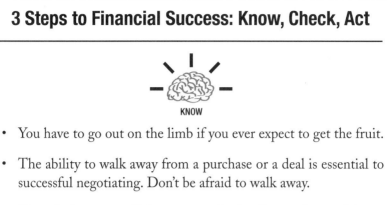

KNOW

- You have to go out on the limb if you ever expect to get the fruit.

- The ability to walk away from a purchase or a deal is essential to successful negotiating. Don't be afraid to walk away.

- Have faith in yourself that you can do this. You really can. It's not hard. All it takes is a simple question to get started: "Is that your best price?"

- Be fair in your pricing and negotiating. The individual selling a product or service has to make money on the transaction, too.

CHECK

- Do your homework: Check every item you want to buy online before going into a retail store.

- Walk into each selling arena knowing the maximum you're willing to pay and the number that's the goal of your negotiations.

ACT

- Believe in yourself and act confidently! Remember, all someone can say to you is "no," and "no" never hurt anyone.

- Remember you can always walk away and come back later if you want to.

"Stop chasing big returns. You can't catch the wind; slow and steady wins the race."

— MATT RETTICK

Chapter 9

Invest Like a Pro
Grow Your Wealth Wisely While Reducing Taxes and Fees

Smart investing is NOT simply about making money. To invest like a pro in today's New Financial Reality, you must learn to grow and protect your money. You also must recognize the right investment and savings opportunities that help defer or eliminate taxes and reduce or avoid fees.

The primary goal of investing and savings, after all, is to provide the income necessary to maintain your Quality of Life Factor (QL) throughout your lifetime.

That's a tall order. But with the help of your true financial advisor and my holistic approach to your personal finances, you can do it.

The Basics

To make the most of the opportunities for true investing success, you must consider your personal goals, devise money strategies with those goals in mind, and make solid investment choices. Your personal tolerance for risk, current financial needs, and peace of mind also must figure into the equation. Remember, this isn't about how to get rich quick—you know what happened to me with that approach! It's about weathering the financial storms of life and succeeding over the long haul with a holistic—whole life—approach to money management.

Think Long Term

Clients repeatedly tell me that my approach to investing their money—thinking long term and with security of principal in mind—has paid off for them, especially with the roller-coaster economy and markets in mind.

Instead of fretting about lost money and broken nest eggs in the stock markets and related investments, today these people are comfortable and secure financially. They traded big ups (and downs) in investment gains for steady increases in their investment without any risk to their principal.

Helen Bratcher is a retired nutritionist, consultant to the U.S. State Department, international director of nutrition, and much more. But, the Tennessean quickly admits, "I'm not a detail person except in my field."

That's why, she says, a number of years ago she heard one of my investment seminars on the importance of financial security without risk and came for help. Now 90, the unstoppable Bratcher recalls, "I just wanted to take my money out of the bank and invest into something that would make more money. I wasn't interested in getting rich or going into the market (Wall Street). I wanted a sound place for my money."

She got that sound investment in the form of annuities. "I've never lost anything, and I'm never worried about money," she adds.

The True You

Too often today, people invest their money in the wrong places without regard to their personal needs or risk tolerances and without an investment plan designed with their QL as the goal.

Business associate David Wilcox, a financial advisor in Palm Beach Gardens, Florida, and co-founder of Prosperity Financial Solutions (www.prosperityfinancialsolutions.com), recounted the story of a client in her 40s. She had been a jockey, but an accident left her disabled and unable to work. She had initially come to him for advice on how to get her investing on track. At the time, her money was invested in high-risk stocks, even though she had a low risk tolerance and her long-term goal was that of a lasting, steady stream of income. A true financial advisor, David helped her understand her real risk tolerance and in turn reinvest her portfolio to ensure she would always have a solid, steady stream of income.

How to Select What's Right for Your Needs

The marketplace is cluttered with dozens of investment approaches and tens of thousands of investment options—from stocks, funds, and bonds to corporate and residential real estate, insurance products, commodities, small-business investments, bank accounts, and multiple combinations of each.

Whatever you and your true financial advisor decide is right for you, keep in mind that your personal investment strategy likely will include several types of investments that, combined, will bring you financial stability and success.

As a grandparent nearing retirement, yet still raising teenagers, I have to focus on saving for my retirement as I continue to work and save. I also need to make sure that my current investments generate enough income to cover the cost of raising teens. It's not easy to combine both, but I'm doing it. To meet the demands of my reality, my money is diversified with security in mind. I'm not heavily invested in international holdings or equities that might risk my principal, and instead have holdings— including annuities—with guaranteed interest rates.

It's important for you, too, to sit down with your true financial advisor and together assemble a winning combination of investments that meet your current and future needs.

What's Your Risk Level?

In Chapter 7, we touched on the importance of personal risk tolerance when it comes to saving for retirement. The concept of tolerance to risk applies to your overall investment strategies and portfolio, too.

Do you lose sleep at night worrying about your investments? You shouldn't if you've invested wisely. You must feel comfortable with an investment, its potential growth, and the security of your principal. If not, then no matter what anyone tells you, the investment is not right for you and your level of risk. Look for an alternative and secure place for your money.

Ups and Downs of a Depressed Market

With the right investments, the daily ups and downs of markets have little, if any, effect on your money. Don't be afraid of down markets; instead, try to understand them.

The reality is that if you buy when prices are lower, you're likely buying the investment on sale, at a discount off the "regular price." That doesn't mean you should take all your cash and buy every stock, bond, piece of real estate, or something else at rock-bottom prices. Counting on a particular stock or piece of real estate to increase in value over time is speculative and risky. You can't count on values to rise in a time frame that suits your investing goals.

Hundreds of thousands of real estate and real estate–related investment speculators learned that lesson firsthand after an exuberant U.S. housing market collapsed into the ongoing foreclosure debacle and left investors desperate to unload over-leveraged properties.

The stock market historically goes up over the (very) long term. But you may be dead long before that happens, and in the interim you must be able to afford to live. I have never owned a pure stock—shares in a single company traded on a stock exchange—in my life. I don't like gambling on the whims of one company. I have invested in a combination of asset classes. Buying and selling individual stocks is simply too insecure an investment strategy for me.

A SAMPLE DIVERSIFIED PORTFOLIO

Here's a classic example of a diversified portfolio invested in a combination of asset classes with safety of principal in mind (percentage of allocation of portfolio):

- Conservative growth fund (10 percent)
- Intermediate-term bond index fund (20 percent)
- Real estate securities fund (10 percent)
- Large-cap growth fund (10 percent)
- Mid-cap growth fund (10 percent)
- Small-cap growth equity (10 percent)
- International equity fund (10 percent)
- Guaranteed return account (20 percent)

Consider the following scenario: The S&P 500 lost 40 percent of its value in 2008. If, on January 1 of that year, you had invested $100,000 in the S&P 500, as of December 31, 2008, your investment would have been worth only $60,000. Not only did you lose $40,000, but what's left of your money will have to work much harder—and it will take much longer—to make up for that $40,000 loss. You now have to try to earn nearly 67 percent of your remaining balance ($60,000) to get your account back up to $100,000! That's what I call "double compounding in reverse." (If you had invested that cash in a fixed-return product instead, your principal—your $100,000—would have been protected.)

Here is the real challenge after a loss like this. If you're young and have years before retirement, you're probably OK. But, what if you were a retiree on a fixed income or nearing retirement when the S&P plummeted? You simply can't recover. You don't have the time. That's precisely what happened to many would-be retirees who find themselves without the money they've counted on for retirement.

> *"Has your broker ever explained what double-compounding in reverse is? I thought not. The bottom line is that regaining big losses can be a steep uphill climb."* —Matt Rettick

My business associate Ron Roberts (Roberts Retirement Group), was at a Wal-Mart near his home east of Sacramento, California, recently when he met a 68-year-old "retiree" who worked 40 hours a week there. The retiree took the job not because he wanted to, but because he had to. The would-be retiree thought he had done everything right for retirement and had invested regularly in his 401(k). The only problem, he had most of his money in his 401(k) invested in the stock market. The man had been poised for retirement in 2008 when the market plummeted. He was left with little choice but to find a job to supplement his lost savings and income.

See the following chart to get a better idea of how difficult it is to make up investment losses.

THE REAL COST OF A MARKET LOSS

If your investment suffers a loss, it requires substantial gains to make up that loss because what's left of your money has to work harder and longer.

Percentage loss on investment	Percentage gain to replace loss
10 percent	11 percent
20 percent	25 percent
30 percent	43 percent
40 percent	67 percent
50 percent	100 percent
60 percent	150 percent
70 percent	233 percent
80 percent	400 percent
90 percent	900 percent
99 percent	9,900 percent

Source: *Index Interest: The Missing Asset Class*, by J.R. Thacker, Chap. 2, p. 16; Resource Media LLC (www.indexinterestbook.com)

Times Change and So Should Your Investments

No matter what you learned growing up, the traditional stalwarts for savings and investing often don't cut it with the New Financial Reality. What was the right way for your dad or grandfather to save isn't necessarily the best approach today.

As an investor, you have endless options for your money, each with pros and cons, pluses and minuses. Before you ever invest a dime, though, know the whole story. Pay close attention to the fees and tax ramifications of any investment, too. They can make a big difference in the value of your portfolio.

Let's examine some traditional and not-so-traditional investment options with safety of principal, and taxes and fee savings in mind.

Beyond Banks

After I started my paper route, I got my first savings account at the local bank. I was 12 when I opened that account, and the bank gave a small "passbook" to record my deposits. It had my name on it, and I felt so grown up because the bank was actually going to pay me money—interest— because I saved money. Back then, banks still were a good place to invest your money. Interest rates on ordinary savings accounts averaged around 6 percent to 8 percent, and your money actually could earn something in the bank over a short period of time.

HOW YOU LOSE MONEY IN THE BANK

Here's how you can lose money annually by leaving large sums of cash in a bank account:

Starting account value: $100,000

Annual interest earned—2 percent (if you're lucky): $2,000

Federal income tax on interest—25 percent (estimated tax bracket): ($500)

State income tax on interest—5 percent (estimated tax bracket): ($100)

Net interest after taxes: $1,400

Net account value after taxes: $101,400

Average inflation rate over last 25 years—3 percent: ($3,042)

Ending purchasing power after 1 year: $98,358

Banks are not the place to park big chunks of your money today. Other than a location for your emergency fund, checking, and small savings, you can't afford it. When you deposit money in savings and money-market accounts, you actually erode your principal because interest rates paid on these accounts are so far below the rate of inflation.

If I had deposited $10,000 in an ordinary savings account at a bank one year ago, today my investment would be worth a little more than $9,800 after factoring in taxes and inflation.

Annuities

In the early 1990s, not long after I started selling health insurance, one of the agencies I was working with brought in a specialist to train us on fixed annuities. Back then, I had no idea what an annuity was. I didn't even know how to spell the word.

The specialist—I still remember his name, Doug Wycoff—was an expert on estate planning strategies, including annuities. Wycoff talked about the history of annuities and thoroughly explained their benefits as a safe money solution with tremendous benefits to the policyholder. After the training session, I was a convert. I still am nearly 30 years later.

Track Record. The concept of annuities dates back to the Roman Empire, when contracts known as *annua* promised a series of payments for a set length of time or for a single payment.

In more modern times, annuities as we now know them surfaced in 1759, when a Pennsylvania company started them for the benefit of Presbyterian ministers and their families.

Over the past 250 plus years, annuities have gone through many changes. But their original premise holds true: favorable accumulation and guaranteed income.

A Simplified Explanation. An annuity is an interest-bearing account or contract, usually with an insurance company, that involves a lump-sum deposit or periodic deposits over a specified length of time. In exchange for the deposit/deposits, the insurance company guarantees immediate or deferred income to the account's owner (the annuitant) or designated beneficiary. Earnings on your principal grow tax deferred and are due only at the time of withdrawal or payout. On the owner's death, any balance that hasn't been withdrawn is paid out to the annuitant's beneficiary either in a lump sum or over time.

ANNUITY BASICS: WHAT IS AN ANNUITY?

- A tax-advantaged interest-bearing account or contract only with an insurance company.

- Insurance company guarantees immediate or deferred income depending on the type of annuity you choose.

FUNDING

- Lump-sum deposit or periodic deposits.

TAXES

- Earnings on principal grow tax deferred.*

- Due only at withdrawal or payout.

DEATH BENEFIT

- Funds in the annuity avoid probate after your death and go directly to beneficiary you name on the annuity application.

PRIMARY TYPES OF ANNUITIES

- **Fixed:** *An account similar to a traditional savings account with a set or declared rate of return.*

- **Indexed:** *Interest earnings tied to the returns of a stock market index like the S&P 500 or Dow Jones Industrial Average or other indices.*

- **Variable:** *Account similar to a mutual fund in which the annuity holder chooses how his or her money will be invested.*

- **Immediate:** *Similar to a traditional pension plan that pays the annuitant (account holder[s]) a set amount of money regularly for a set amount of time (can be for life).*

For more details on the pros and cons of various types of annuities, visit www.ChecksandBalances.TV and download your free report.

Excludes immediate annuities

Triple Compounding. Annuities can be a great investment opportunity, in part because of the "miracle" of what I call triple compounding interest. Fixed, fixed indexed, and variable annuities earn this triple compounding interest. Your initial investment or principal earns interest; your interest earns interest, and the dollars you would have paid in taxes earn interest.

> *The great 20th century mathematician Albert Einstein called compounding interest the eighth wonder of the world.*

I'm not alone in liking annuities. As of last year, more than $2 trillion was invested in annuities in the United States alone. The U.S. General Accounting Office even recommends Americans invest in annuities as a way to ensure they don't outlive their savings (www.gao.gov/assets/320/319396.pdf).

Fixed and Variable. With a fixed, fixed indexed, and variable annuity, a client pays no front-end loads (fees) or commissions. Further, these annuities offer a guaranteed death benefit and the opportunity to convert this accumulating asset into an income stream you cannot outlive.

Bonds

Bonds come in all varieties—from ultra-secure U.S. government-issued bonds to high-risk mortgage-backed bonds. When you purchase a bond of any kind you, the investor, are loaning your money to that entity for a set time in exchange for a set or variable rate of return.

Rates on bonds tend to move opposite interest rates. If interest rates drop, the rates on bonds go up, and conversely. Because they are so secure, bonds pay some of the lowest interest rates. But bonds, especially broadly diversified bond funds, can play an essential role in the stability of a portfolio. And, because a fund is made up of so many bonds, the default of any one bond doesn't impact the overall portfolio.

Bond interest is generally taxed as ordinary income, though not all bonds are subject to federal income tax. State and municipal bonds enjoy special tax treatment—their interest is exempt from federal income tax.

Additionally, if a bond is issued by the state in which you live, it's state income tax free, too. Be careful, however, if you're nearing retirement age. All of your municipal bond interest income is included in determining whether any of your Social Security income will be taxed.

No-Load Mutual Funds

A mutual fund is a group of holdings in a minimum of 20 different investments. It could be stocks, bonds, other mutuals, or any combination. The right mutual fund—one carefully selected with the fund's stated goal, your goals, and your degree of investment risk in mind—provides instant diversity in one place, and can have the opportunity for increased portfolio growth.

Fund fees (loads) can be high. Look for no-load funds—with no fees paid when you buy or sell the fund. Mutual funds all charge annual management fees and other transaction costs. Those costs can include 12b-1 fees, which are not disclosed in your monthly statement (you'll have to dig it out of the company's prospectus) and usually are charged against your account to provide money for the company to advertise and promote the fund. Transaction costs aren't easy to identify either; they relate to how often the fund manager buys and sells assets within the fund every year. (Visit www.PersonalFund.com to find out the transaction fees associated with a mutual fund.)

Pay attention to the tax ramifications of a mutual fund, too. Every year—even in a losing year—a mutual fund must report its profits made from selling securities for that year. Those gains are paid to shareholders either in income dividends or capital gains, and shareholders must pay taxes on those gains.

People opt to buy mutual funds generally because they're managed by trained professionals. The performance of those professional investment managers, however, is measured against an unmanaged index with the same types of investments—the S&P Index, for example.

Check out the free online mutual fund Expense Analyzer from FINRA, the non-governmental Financial Industry Regulatory Authority (http://cxa.marketwatch.com/finra/MutualFund/AdvancedScreener/AdvancedScreener.aspx).

Indexed Funds

An indexed fund is an alternative to an ordinary mutual fund, but without the hefty fees. It's an unmanaged fund that mirrors various stock indices and therefore can provide diversity. If structured properly, an index fund can help insulate your investments against the ups and downs of a particular industry.

An indexed fund buys the same stocks in the same proportion as its underlying index so that its performance usually mirrors the index minus whatever the fund charges in management fees—usually a very low 0.5 percent.

When it comes to paying for an actively managed fund—a typical mutual fund—the real question is: "Can the professionally managed mutual fund generate better returns than the broad index (and index fund)?" Scores of "experts" and books will tell you that the answer is, "no." You can easily check out the track records of various funds online at Morningstar Inc. (www.morningstar.com).

Exchanged-Traded Funds

Exchange-traded funds (ETFs) are a cross between a mutual fund and a stock. They are a basket of other investments so they offer diversification to offset the risk of buying an individual stock. They are not actively managed like a mutual fund and can mirror an index like the S&P 500 (the Spider/SPDR). But they have lower costs and generally are more tax efficient than mutual funds.

Unlike a mutual fund, ETFs can be bought and sold throughout the trading day and are continually priced like stocks. Because they have less turnover—buying and selling—in their portfolio of holdings, that means less capital gains (or losses) and fewer taxes that you, the investment owner, must pay. You don't pay taxes on the earnings on your ETF holdings until *you* sell those holdings.

On the downside, ETFs, like mutual funds, may also charge some type of buy or sell commissions/fees, though they are normally much lower than a mutual fund.

Unit Investment Trust

Another unmanaged diverse investment is a unit investment trust, or UIT. Because it's unmanaged, it normally has lower costs compared with mutual funds. But UITs do have sales fees.

A UIT buys a basket of assets one at a time when the trust is created, and then sells shares of the trust to investors. Typically, UITs have a set offering period, a set number of units offered, and a termination date when the UIT dissolves and proceeds are paid to its investors.

Like mutual funds, UIT holders must pay income taxes on dividends, interest, and capital gains/losses distributed to them. However, some UITs—made up of tax-free bonds, for example—can be federal and/or state tax free.

Cut Your Tax Bite Now

Everyone knows the saying, "Nothing is certain in life but death and taxes." Both are inevitable. However, each of us monitors our health and does what we can to live as long as possible. We should be just as diligent in monitoring the amount of taxes we pay and do what we can to limit our tax liabilities within the law. No one wants to die young, and no one wants to pay more taxes than required, either.

You must work with your true financial advisor to allocate your investments to limit your tax bite. Consider more tax-advantaged investments. An unmanaged fund or ETFs and UITs, for example, as I mentioned above, can have minimal portfolio turnover and subsequently fewer capital gains—and taxes on those capital gains—due on an annual basis. Some other tax-efficient investments include mutual funds with low turnover rates, municipal bonds, and fixed and indexed CDs.

Scam Alert!

We've all heard it so many times, "If it sounds too good to be true, it probably is!" Yet, good people continually are fooled by professional scam artists and their Ponzi schemes. No one is immune to or safe from these masters of deception.

The rich and famous, as well as the uneducated AND higher educated, have been trapped by the web of "guaranteed" higher returns and "no risk" investment promises made by these shysters. These people are gregarious, outgoing, and magnetic speakers who mesmerize their audiences with their charm, knowledge, and seemingly inside connections to the underworld of high finance. That's exactly what happened to me time and again before my financial epiphany. The smooth talk and slick sales pitches sucked me into the get-rich-quick scams and schemes, and they all failed.

The worst part of the scam is that many times you're introduced to these people by friends and family members or church and synagogue leaders. You believe in the person who introduced you, so naturally you believe in the scam artist's story of a richer return on your money just around the corner. Of course, in most cases, these good people themselves have been duped.

You're gullible as well, because we all at some point in our lives chase greed. We think the get-rich-quick schemes really do work. It took me years to realize they don't. Plus, as investors, everyone wants a higher return on their money. I learned the hard way that financial freedom takes careful planning and steady investing and saving. I hope you can learn that, too.

You never know where and how a scam will hit you. Several years ago, a lady in her 70s came to us very upset. It seems she had been taken for $25,000 in a Nigerian scam. Someone had called her to say that one of her relatives had left her a large sum of money. In order to receive the cash she would have to set up an account. The distraught woman ended up sending thousands of dollars to cover "taxes, fees, and processing," and, of course, losing it all in the process.

Keys to Protect Yourself

Here are a few suggestions on how you can protect yourself from scams and schemes:

- Don't trust anyone's word as gospel—even friends or family. Keep your guard up at all times, and take the Checks and Balances approach. Weigh the pros AND cons of every investment.

- When considering any financial product, call the state insurance department (if it's an insurance product), or the SEC (if it's a securities product), and ask if the product is registered, legal, and approved in your state. Also, check out your broker with FINRA by logging onto www.brokercheck.com.

- Before you hand over anything, call your local Better Business Bureau to find out if a company is registered and if any complaints have been filed against the company by unhappy investors.

- Call the state attorney general's office and ask about the particular product or investment. Is the office aware of the investment? Have there been any investigations into the product or company? If so, steer clear.

- Never hand over cash or write a check in the name of the salesman or financial advisor who is promoting the investment or to their own company. Make your check payable to the institution, insurance company, or brokerage firm that is underwriting the product or investment.

- Never give out your personal information via the Internet or over the telephone. If someone wants additional information from you, contact the company directly to confirm the legitimacy of the request.

- And, of course, go with your gut and intuition. "If it sounds too good to be true, it probably is."

- Make sure your monthly investment statements do not come from the individual advisor's office or on his or her letterhead. The statements always should originate from a third-party custodian like TD Ameritrade or Pershing, or a brokerage firm like Merrill Lynch or Edward Jones, or an insurance company.

Organizations Designed to Protect You

Plenty of government, industry, and private organizations are charged with protecting investors from fraud. If you think you've been conned or are suspicious of an investment or advisor, do your due diligence, and don't hesitate to contact the appropriate agency. Some of those agencies include:

- Federal Deposit Insurance Corporation (www.FDIC.gov)
- Federal Reserve (www.FederalReserve.gov)
- Federal Trade Commission (www.FTC.gov)
- Financial Industry Regulatory Authority (www.FINRA.org)
- Securities and Exchange Commission (www.SEC.gov)
- Securities Investors Protection Corporation (www.SIPC.org)

Checks and Balances Tools

Download or read our free reports at www.ChecksandBalances.TV:

- The Truth About Wall Street
- The Truth About Mutual Funds
- The Truth About Stocks
- The Truth About Bonds
- The Truth About Banks
- The Truth About Exchange-Traded Funds
- The Truth About Annuities: Immediate, Fixed, Indexed, and Variable
- The Truth About Investment Fees, Charges, and Loads
- The Truth About How to Become a 21st Century Investor
- The Truth About Ponzi Schemes, Scams, and Blue Sky: How to Protect Yourself from the Next Round of "Too Good to Be True" Investments

Download our free checklists at www.ChecksandBalances.TV to use before buying any major purchase or investment:

- Stocks
- Bonds
- Mutual funds
- Annuities
- ETFs
- Life insurance
- Disability insurance

3 Steps to Financial Success: Know, Check, Act

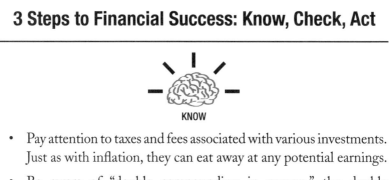

KNOW

- Pay attention to taxes and fees associated with various investments. Just as with inflation, they can eat away at any potential earnings.

- Be aware of "double compounding in reverse," the double whammy of losing money in the market. Not only are you out your former account balance, but your remaining account balance must now work even harder to gain back the losses.

- Beware of scams. If you think something isn't right, don't hesitate to contact the appropriate regulatory or monitoring agency.

CHECK

- Ask yourself and your spouse/significant other if you're losing sleep at night worrying about your investments. If so, you're in the wrong investments!

- Figure out how much money (percentage-wise) that you have in the bank. If it's more than 20 percent of your total liquid assets, you're losing a lot of buying power due to inflation.

ACT

- Always move cautiously when considering any investment. It can take you a lifetime to save up a nice nest egg and only a moment to lose it all.

- Contact your local regulatory departments if you ever have any questions about a product or investment.

"I'm not so much interested in the return ON my money, as I am in the return OF my money."

— WILL ROGERS

Chapter 10

Stop Losing Money in the Market
Capture Your Gains With Indexed CDs, Annuities, and Universal Life Insurance

magine investing your money so that it remains safe from losses no matter the volatility of the economy or the markets around it. Your investment is unequivocally protected, no questions asked. Even with today's roller-coaster stock markets, this isn't a pipe dream. It's reality with indexed interest assets, including indexed CDs, indexed fixed annuities, and indexed universal life insurance.

Each type of investment allows you to share in the upside of the stock market, while your principal is protected on the downside. The bottom line: Your money is safeguarded against losses.

A Primer

Indexed interest products aren't new. Adjustable-rate mortgages and some credit-card interest rates have utilized the concept for years. Rates go up when the prime rate climbs, and down when it drops, with limitations on both the upside and downside.

Indexed interest assets link their rate of return to the performance of a particular stock or bond index, like the S&P 500, the Dow Jones Industrial Average, or the 10-year U.S. Treasury bond index. When the underlying index gains ground, your earnings on the investment grow.

When the index falls, your principal (plus any annual earnings already locked in) are 100 percent protected.

Upside Gains

Remember the 2008 scenario with the S&P 500 I mentioned in the last chapter? That year the S&P lost 37 percent of its value. If, at the beginning of 2008, you had invested your money in an indexed interest asset that tracks the S&P, at the end of that year, you would have lost *nothing*!

Consider the numbers. Let's say you started the year with a $10,000 investment in the stocks in the S&P 500. Instead of ending 2008 with only $6,700—your $10,000 would have remained intact.

It sounds too good to be true. Yet it absolutely is true. The hundreds of billions of dollars already invested in these kinds of indexed interest assets are a testament to that. Last year alone, investors bought $32 billion in fixed indexed annuities.

The Tradeoff

There is a downside—sort of. With these types of indexed interest assets, your investment normally earns slightly less than the actual gains of its underlying index—it varies, but generally 30 percent to 70 percent of the gain. Almost always the percentage of gains you could earn annually are capped, too. You also do not receive any dividends from the stocks in the underlying index.

Potential investors may cringe at the thought of not getting ALL the gains "due" them. But consider what you get in exchange for giving up a percentage of the gains: We often forget that when an investment drops in value, the remaining money must work that much harder to make up for the loss. For example, if you invest that $100,000 in a mutual fund and it drops 25 percent in one year, you're left with a $75,000 investment. In order to make up the $25,000 loss in principal, the remaining $75,000 will have to grow a full 34 percent, or a third of its current value, in order for your investment to return to $100,000.

Taking those numbers into consideration, the cost of an index interest asset is a small tradeoff for the tremendous security of your money. If you doubt that, ask a few of the would-be retirees with nest eggs in 401(k) plans who fell victim to the Great Recession of 2008–2009 and now find themselves still hard at work because they can no longer afford to retire. If they had invested their money in index interest assets, their principal along with any previous years' gains would have remained intact and many of them would be happily retired now.

Would you rather an investment have the potential for a 100 percent gain on your money AND a 100 percent loss, or a 50 percent gain on your money and 0 percent loss? That's a no-brainer. We all would prefer no losses!

INTEREST INDEXED ASSETS

Here are several types of indexed interest assets along with a few of their pros and cons:

- **Fixed Indexed Annuities:** Guaranteed fixed minimum interest rate of return; potential for greater gains depending on performance of underlying index; principal and previous annual gains locked in every year and protected from loss due to market declines. **Disadvantage:** Withdrawals other than specified in contract may carry a penalty.

- **Indexed Universal Life Insurance:** Policy owner shares in a limited portion of market gains while principal protected from losses; includes a guaranteed minimum interest rate on each policy; includes tax-advantaged death benefit for heirs. Cash withdrawals generally are income tax free as long as amount of withdrawals does not exceed value of premiums paid to date. **Disadvantage:** Interest rate caps limit market gains.

- **Indexed CDs:** A certificate of deposit in which its interest rate of return is linked to the performance of an underlying market index like the S&P 500 or Dow Jones Industrial Average; principal insured by agency of the federal government. **Disadvantage:** Restrictions on early withdrawals; interest earnings are not tax deferred so income taxes due on gains every year.

Let's look more closely at the three primary types of index-linked assets. All three offer protection for your principal.

Fixed Indexed Annuities

Finally, there is an investment linked to stock market gains that's absolutely safe from a stock market loss! A fixed indexed annuity is an annuity contract with an insurance company that carries a guaranteed fixed minimum interest rate of return and ties the possibility of additional gains to an equities index like the S&P 500.

Depending on how gains are credited to your particular annuity, if the S&P 500 goes up 4 percent in one year, you could gain all or a part of that 4 percent increase. If it goes down, you lose nothing. Your earnings are flat for that year, but your principal *and* previous gains are locked in. As far as I know, this is the only account in America that locks in any gain you realize on your policy anniversary date. You lose nothing. It's all about the power of zero.

With a fixed indexed annuity, you're not invested directly in the stock market or in the underlying index. Instead, you own an insurance policy with gains on the investment linked to returns of a market index. But, if the index drops sharply, you do not lose your money—guaranteed.

Underlying Indexes

Fixed indexed annuities can be linked to any number of indices and can be made up of stocks, bonds, industries, and more. The most common, however, is the S&P 500. That index is a compilation of stocks of the 500 largest companies in the United States and represents every major industry in the economy. As such, it's a broad measure of our stock market and the overall economy.

When It Makes Sense

Fixed indexed annuities can be a great alternative to owning a typically conservative product like bonds because they offer more upside growth potential plus have additional benefits—including the guaranteed security. You the consumer can't lose your principal or locked-in interest due to market volatility.

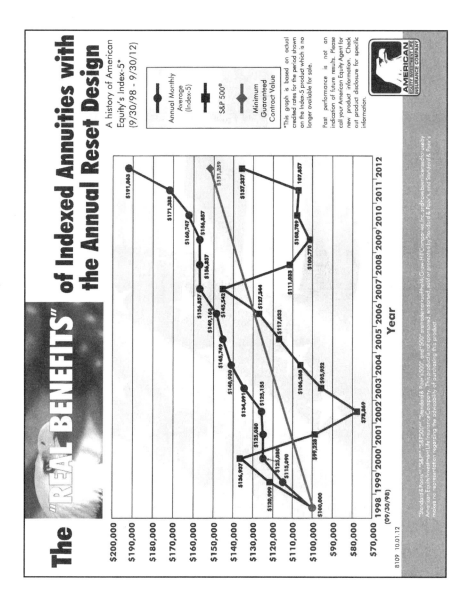

The ability to provide you future income to combat inflation or supplement retirement is another big plus of these investments. Many fixed indexed annuities allow the income value of the contract to compound annually at 6 percent.

Watch Your Money Grow

Remember, with an annuity, your investment grows tax deferred. Taxes on the earnings are due only at time of withdrawal or payout. Meanwhile, watch your money capitalize on that power of triple compounding—your initial investment or principal earns interest; your interest earns interest, and the dollars you would have paid in taxes earn interest.

> *"With an index-linked account in a down market you truly can say, 'Zero is my hero.'"* —Matt Rettick

On the annuity owner's death, any balance that hasn't been withdrawn is paid out to the annuitant's beneficiary either in a lump sum or over time.

Access to Your Funds

With most annuities, your money is readily accessible if you need it. An annuity isn't as liquid as money in a checking, savings, or money-market account. But you can access up to usually 10 percent of your account balance per year without any penalties. Above 10 percent you normally incur what's known as a surrender charge. The good news is that those surrender charges decline over time. Surrender charges also can be waived if the annuity owner dies, gets sick and needs to go into a nursing home, or if he or she is diagnosed with a terminal illness.

Benefit Riders

Fixed indexed annuities come in all types and configurations. One of the more recent versions is a fixed indexed annuity with a **lifetime income benefit rider (LIBR).** These riders can have no fees or a fee of up to 1.25 percent per year. In return, LIBRs generally offer a guaranteed growth rate on your account value (5 percent to 7 percent) as well as a guaranteed withdrawal rate for your lifetime based on a specific formula (4 percent to 6 percent).

There is no such thing as a "typical" LIBR because each insurance company offers its own unique benefits associated with the rider. It's important to read the fine print and make sure you fully understand all aspects of any potential rider you're considering.

Understanding the Disadvantages

The main disadvantage of fixed indexed annuities is that the annuity owner receives no dividends on the stocks that make up the policy's underlying index. It's part of the tradeoff for the investment's ironclad security guarantee. In addition, if you withdraw any interest earnings in a calendar year, they are taxed at your ordinary income tax rate—not at capital gains tax rate.

There also can be early withdrawal penalties from the IRS if you take any withdrawals prior to age 59½. However, it's possible to limit fees and/or penalties with the right strategies, so it's important to work with your true financial advisor who understands the ins and outs of these insurance products.

Indexed Universal Life Insurance

Indexed life insurance is yet another approach to investing that allows you to share in a portion of the upside of booming markets while protecting your principal from plummeting markets. Not only does the insurance company assume all of the downside risk, it also provides a guaranteed minimum interest rate on each policy.

In exchange for the security of your money, you trade off some of the gains in the investment. Generally, interest rates paid on a policy are capped. Additionally, if your cash withdrawals exceed the total value of your premiums paid into the policy, there can be tax ramifications.

If a policyholder misses premium payments—the "grace period" or number of missed payments varies by insurer—a policy can lapse. However, most companies allow the policyholder to make up missed payments and reinstate the policy and the benefits.

Plenty of Shapes and Sizes

Indexed universal life comes in plenty of varieties. Different companies offer differing caps, minimum guarantees, and participation rates. Some even include no-lapse protection guarantees on the death benefit portion of the contract.

Consider a typical indexed universal life insurance policy and what it means in terms of benefits to its policyholder and his heirs: A 45-year-old male—I'll call him Tom—buys an $850,000 indexed universal life insurance policy that requires him to pay $15,000 a year in premiums until he reaches age 65. (If Tom dies during that time, his heirs will receive the full $850,000 death benefit, no matter how much money he has or hasn't paid into the account.) At age 65, Tom stops paying premiums and, if he chooses, can begin receiving an income-tax-free lifetime income of $25,000 a year. His policy's death benefit also starts to increase. If Tom dies at age 75, for example, the income-tax-free death benefit will have grown to $1.5 million.

What if Tom had deposited $20,000 per year? His investment would be that much larger and more impressive, both in terms of tax-free income and the amount of the death benefit to his heirs.

When It Makes Sense

Determining whether indexed universal life insurance makes sense for you isn't a simple "yes" or "no." The answer depends on your needs and wants. Are you considering the investment for the purpose of income or to provide a death benefit for your heirs, or both?

As an investment, indexed universal life has the tax-deferred growth benefits of Roth IRAs and can be a good fit for someone who earns too much money to qualify for a Roth IRA.

These policies also can be a tax-advantaged way to build your savings, while still providing the opportunity to withdraw some or all of your money as needed later in life, and to provide your heirs a tax-free benefit if you pass away.

Tax Issues

Generally, policy withdrawals are income tax free as long as they do not exceed the value of premiums paid to date. If they do exceed the value of the premiums paid in, they are taxed as ordinary income.

However, with most policies it's possible to take cash withdrawals as "policy loans." Policy loans do not have to be repaid while the policyholder is alive. Any outstanding loans plus interest not repaid at the policyholder's death are deducted from the death benefit to heirs.

This type of insurance can be an ideal investment for someone who wants to make taxes work for them.

Indexed CDs

A certificate of deposit, or CD, is an interest-bearing time deposit that promises a certain return on your lump sum investment if held to maturity. It's low risk and your principal is FDIC-insured. An indexed CD—they go by a variety of names—differs from an ordinary CD in that its interest rate of return is linked to the performance of an underlying market index like the S&P 500 or Dow Jones Industrial Average rather than a fixed interest rate. It can be an excellent way to grow your money without increased risk, and is another good alternative to ordinary bond investments.

As with its indexed asset cousins—indexed annuities and indexed universal life—if the underlying index goes up, generally so does the interest rate on the indexed CD. If the index declines, however, your principal remains protected. Some indexed CDs also will guarantee a minimum interest rate if the CD is held to maturity.

Advantages

Indexed CDs can provide the best of both worlds—participation in the upside gains of the stock market combined with the security of your principal insured by an agency of the federal government (FDIC). They also do not have annual management fees. They're a good alternative to and have more security than a typical bond investment.

If you don't need annual interest as income paid regularly to you— indexed CDs don't pay out their interest earnings until their maturity— and want better rates than with traditional CDs, these indexed CDs can be a good fit for your portfolio.

But as with any investment, you must pay attention to the details. Those details can relate to everything from withdrawals and fees, to penalties, and even how interest rates are determined. All this varies by issuer and by product, too.

Disadvantages

Indexed CDs generally are created to be held to maturity so your money is tied up for a specific period of time.

They can carry hefty fees and restrictions, so shop carefully. Some products do not always allow access to your principal without penalty charges prior. to the maturity date. Other products limit the access for certain time periods—usually in the early stages of the investment. Earnings generally are capped, too.

Also, keep in mind that the interest that you earn on your investment is taxed as ordinary income every year. It's not tax deferred like an indexed annuitiy. The interest rate you earn on an indexed CD also may be calculated by sometimes complex formulas determined by the issuer.

Checks and Balances Tools

Download or read our free reports at www.ChecksandBalances.TV:

- The Truth About Fixed Indexed Annuities
- The Truth About Average Stock Market Returns
- The Truth About Protecting Your Nest Egg from Market Downturns

3 Steps to Financial Success: Know, Check, Act

KNOW

- Fixed indexed annuities—because of their tax-deferred growth status—provide a great way to grow your money through triple compounding.

- Indexed universal life insurance allows your money to grow in a tax-advantaged manner while still providing a death benefit to your heirs, as well as tax-free withdrawals during your retirement.

- Indexed CDs can provide the best of both worlds—participation in the upside gains of the stock market combined with the security of your principal insured by the U.S. government.

CHECK

- Ask your current advisor if he or she can offer you fixed indexed annuities, indexed universal life insurance, and indexed CDs. If not, find a new financial advisor.

- Look for an indexed annuity that offers a lifetime income benefit rider to guarantee an income stream for life.

ACT

- Take control of your financial future by asking your current or next advisor the tough questions we suggest in our "10 Questions to Ask Your Financial Advisor *Before* You Invest a Dime With Them."

"The old fear of dying shortly after retirement has been replaced with the fear of outliving your money."

— MATT RETTICK

Chapter 11

Solving Longevity
How to Guarantee Your Money Lasts as Long as You Do!

Watching my grandparents waste away penniless and at the dictates of governmental rules and regulations was one of the hardest things I've ever endured. As a young man, I was powerless—and without the cash—to help.

Had they planned ahead; had they saved the right way; had they invested even small amounts with the goal of creating an income stream for life; and had they purchased long-term-care insurance or an equivalent, their so-called golden years would have been very different. My grandparents would have had choices and options concerning their care, their later years could have been more comfortable, and they and their loved ones—myself and my family included—would have been much happier.

You have the option now of making a difference for yourself down the road.

"Delayed gratification doesn't pay off until you arrive in the future." —Matt Rettick

---

It's the Rest of Your Life!

True financial freedom means financial security for the rest of your life, including your retirement years. If you ignore your retirement and don't build the financial foundation to support yourself in the future, you will fall short of the goal.

> *At retirement, if people plan their finances to cover their basic economic needs throughout the remainder of their expected lifetime—roughly age 86—half of them can be expected to fail. The reason: Half will live longer, and many much longer, than the average life expectancy.*
>
> **Source:** "Investing Your Lump Sum at Retirement," an essay by David F. Babbel and Craig B. Merrill, Wharton Financial Institutions Center, Wharton School of the University of Pennsylvania (http://fic. wharton.upenn.edu/fic/policy%20page/whartonessay18.pdf)

Adding to the pressure, Americans are living longer. That means your money must last longer, too. In fact, nonagenarians—age 90 and up— are the fastest growing segment of the U.S. senior population, the U.S. Census Bureau reports.

We must prepare financially for our longevity. It doesn't take huge sums of money. But it does take a conscious effort to plan properly so your money doesn't run out before you die. I've talked to and worked with hundreds of retirees over the years, and all of them—even those who are wealthy—worry that their money will run out before they die.

> *Outliving their money is the biggest fear of 61 percent of Baby Boomers today!*
> — *"Reclaiming the Future," a 2010 study from Allianz Life Insurance Company of North America*

Short on Time

As we age, the two things that used to work in our financial favor—time and earned income from our job or business—now begin to work against us. Unfortunately, this can really hurt retirees and pre-retirees if they don't plan properly.

When you're young and working, you can better afford the wild fluctuations of the stock market. You have ample time to allow the markets to recover from any losses and to watch your investment grow, while you live off your wages from your employer or the profits from your business.

But when you near your 60s, 70s, and 80s, time is *not* on your side. You generally don't have any income from an employer. That's why it's essential to utilize and pay attention to the "Investment Rule of 100."

"The Investment Rule of 100," if you remember from Chapter 7, states that you subtract your current age from 100—your potential longevity—and invest the remainder, expressed as a percentage, in higher-risk accounts. The rest of your money should be in investments that offer some growth, but still protect your principal.

The Truth About What the Government Will Pay

Too many people shrug off longevity planning with the comment, "I can always just live off the government." As I can attest, that's a gut-wrenching approach to aging for you and your loved ones. It's not enough anymore, either. You want better choices, and you can have them.

It's Not Automatic

If you think that relying on the government to pay for nursing-home care is the best option for you in your later years, you seriously need to think again.

Do you really want the government to dictate where and how you will be cared for? If you haven't planned ahead financially, you could be out of luck and out of pocket potentially large sums of money that could drain your resources until nothing is left for you or your loved ones. In addition, many people don't realize that Medicaid pays for nursing-home care for qualified individuals only, and Medicare pays only a portion of medical care for the elderly with limitations and co-pays.

What happens if Medicaid and Medicare go bust? It's a real possibility, considering the New Financial Reality and how it has hit federal and state governments with massive budget deficits.

Suppose you don't need nursing-home care, but do need help? Not everyone ends up in a nursing home in their later years. At some point in their later years, however, most people do require assistance with daily living in some form—whether it's home-health care, an in-home aide, or assisted living. The government—Medicare or Medicaid—does NOT cover that care long term. Medicare reimburses qualified recipients in some cases for a *limited* time following a hospital stay. But that's it. Otherwise, you're on your own. Either you pay for the help, someone you know pays for the help, or you struggle along without it.

As I mentioned earlier, when my Grandma Wick became ill with Alzheimer's, my Aunt Lorna moved in to help her in Detroit. My grandmother didn't have much savings, and no one wanted her to be in a nursing home. Eventually, as my grandmother's condition worsened, my Aunt Lorna moved her back to New Jersey with her. My mother still remembers how rough those years as a full-time caregiver were for my aunt.

Do You Want to Be Destitute?

Medicaid isn't exactly jumping at the chance to foot the bill for anyone, either. To meet eligibility requirements for Medicaid, you'll have to spend down almost all your assets. (There are certain exemptions, including allowing a spouse to keep his or her home and limited resources.) You can give away your assets or transfer them to your kids, but those steps require long-term planning. Medicaid rules require states to "look back" at someone's finances for five years prior to the date that person *files for* Medicaid to make sure he or she didn't dump assets solely to qualify for free care. If you're married, both spouses' assets are pooled for purposes of the look-back. (For more on Medicaid eligibility rules, visit www.cms.gov/MedicaidEligibility/.)

For these reasons plus your peace of mind and your loved ones' peace of mind, and to maintain the financial freedom you've worked so hard to achieve, you must plan financially now for your later years so your money doesn't run out.

Chances are you and I have many years ahead of us. Considering the soaring costs of health care and all the other expenses connected with aging, your retirement will take some doing.

What About Social Security?

Traditionally, Americans looked ahead to their retirement and figured company defined-benefit pension plans and Social Security would take care of them for life. No one paid much attention to Social Security benefit planning or the ups and downs of various markets. After all, the company and the government would take care of them.

Then came the onslaught of defined contribution plans like 401(k)s, and suddenly your retirement security was up to you, and market swings made all the difference. Further upsetting longevity planning, Social Security was (and still is) in trouble, and companies began pulling the plugs on or underfunding many of the remaining defined-benefit plans.

DEFINED-BENEFIT PLAN PAYOUT

If you're among the dwindling number of people lucky enough to have an employer who still offers a (traditional) defined-benefit retirement plan, make sure you elect the joint-life or spousal-survivor payout option if you're married. That will ensure that monthly income payments will continue if you die prior to your spouse.

The bottom line today: Funding your retirement is up to *you*. You can't count on Social Security. Even if it's around when you need it, it's still not going to be enough to fund your retirement. You simply must plan ahead, and that includes how and when you will take your Social Security benefits. All of this does make a BIG difference in your financial security and longevity planning.

A Strained System

We're constantly reminded that Social Security is running out of money. But that's not its biggest problem. What's really wrong with Social Security is that the system has to take care of too many people for too long a time. That's not what it was designed to do. When then-President

Franklin Delano Roosevelt started Social Security in 1935, the average life expectancy in America was just over 61 years. Because it's an average, which means that some people died before age 61 and some beyond age 61, the Social Security system was only designed to fund individual retirement for a few years.

Fast forward to today. With our increasing life spans, some Americans are retired—and looking to Social Security for support—for more years than they actually worked and paid into the system. Factor in the massive numbers of beginning-to-retire Baby Boomers, and the already taxed system becomes overwhelmed to the breaking point. In 2011 alone, the Social Security system paid out $45 billion more in benefits and administrative costs than it received in non-interest (tax) income (www.ssa.gov/oact/trsum/index.html.)

Social Security reform is inevitable and will eventually happen. It's also likely that this reform will create a much different system for future generations.

Election Strategies

Until reform happens, Social Security remains a guaranteed, inflation-adjusted, tax-preferred, lifetime income stream. Would-be retirees should plan carefully, though, how and when they elect to take their benefits. Making the wrong choice can leave thousands of dollars (potential income) on the table.

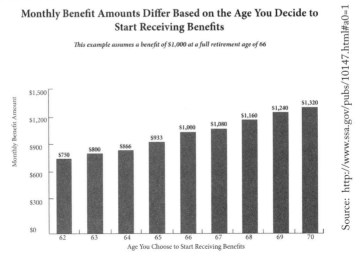

Monthly Benefit Amounts Differ Based on the Age You Decide to Start Receiving Benefits

This example assumes a benefit of $1,000 at a full retirement age of 66

Source: http://www.ssa.gov/pubs/10147.html#a0=1

154

For example, if your full benefit at age 66 amounts to $1,000 a month, and you chose to retire at age 62 instead, you would receive an income of $750 a month plus inflation adjustments for the rest of your life. If instead of electing to begin receiving your benefits at age 62, you chose not to take your benefits until age 70, you then would be eligible to receive $1,320 a month plus inflation adjustments for the rest of your life. Over 10 years, that $570 a month in extra income adds up to $68,400 that you passed up.

When you elect to take your Social Security benefits depends on a number of things, including your need for income, the ability of your investment portfolio to bridge any income gaps, and the election strategies available to you. Married couples, divorced couples, and widows/widowers have various options that can enhance their income situations. For example, if you're divorced, you may qualify for what can amount to substantial Social Security benefits from a former spouse.

For more on Social Security elections, consult with your true financial advisor, and check out more information on the Social Security website (www.ssa.gov) and visit PlanMyBenefit.com (www.PlanMyBenefit.com).

Your Private Pension Plan

We all know it takes more than Social Security to create your sound financial future. With defined-benefit retirement plans disappearing and defined-contribution plans like 401(k)s falling victim to big market

---

WHAT AMERICANS LOOK FOR IN A RETIREMENT INVESTMENT

Following are the top five attributes of financial products as rated by respondents in a survey* by Allianz Life Insurance Company of North America:

- Stable, predictable retirement standard of living.

- Guaranteed income stream for life.

- Guaranteed not to lose value.

- Protection against market downside.

- Don't need to think about it; stable and predictable.

Source: "Reclaiming the Future," 2010; www.retirementmadesimpler.org/Library/ENT-991.pdf

---

losses, it's doubly important for Americans to look to other options to finance their longevity.

Combating Stock Market Volatility

"Buy and hold stocks and mutual funds" may have been a mantra for many people before the New Financial Reality. But the results of that investment strategy have turned into financial nightmares and delayed retirements today.

In the wake of 401(k) plans and nest eggs wiped out by plummeting markets twice in the last decade, the new emphasis for retirement investments is on guaranteed income streams for life. The downturns have been a wake-up call for all of us.

One of my Nashville clients, Matthew Kennedy, came to one of my investment seminars more than a dozen years ago. He was a teacher who had retired from Fisk University with a modest 403(b) plan invested in the stock market, and he was concerned about his financial future. Even though he had regularly put aside what he thought was enough money, Matthew worried that he didn't have enough to maintain his modest quality of life in his later years.

Though his lifestyle was far from extravagant, this middle-income American—like so many others today—was afraid he would outlive his money because of the volatility of the markets.

I worked with Matthew and helped him with a fixed annuity that pays him a monthly income for the rest of his life. Matthew says he was attracted to the concept of a fixed annuity because he could begin drawing from it almost immediately—at the time, he had already retired. The interest rate compared favorably with then-current rates, too, and was much more than what the banks were paying. "I was content to sit back and watch my account grow with no worries that my money would run out before I die," Matthew, now 91, says.

Matthew remains secure in his future, and it's gratifying for me to know that someone who worked so hard and did so much for his community can live out his life with financial freedom.

The Value of a Guaranteed Income Stream

Ten years ago, Jack Miller and his wife, Anne Riley Miller, also from Nashville, came to me very concerned about their investment portfolio. At the time, it was dominated by stock-based investments and subject to market volatility. Jack was an orthopedic surgeon nearing retirement, and Anne was worried that they needed to change their investment approach in order to preserve their QL in retirement. It was a wise concern on her part.

RECOMMENDATIONS FROM THE GAO

A U.S. Government Accountability Office report suggests that retirees consider some of the following options (actual choices will depend on your individual circumstances—anticipated expenses, income level, health, tolerance for risk, and more):

- Systematically draw down your savings and convert a portion into an income annuity to cover necessary expenses.

- Opt for an annuity provided by an employer-sponsored defined-benefit pension rather than a lump sum withdrawal.

- Delay receipt of Social Security benefits until at least your full retirement age, and in some cases, continue to work and save.

The GAO profiled two middle-net-wealth households ($350,000 to $375,000 net wealth). Experts recommended the following scenario:

- Purchase annuities with a portion of savings.

- Draw down savings at an annual rate—4 percent of the initial balance.

- Use lifetime income from a defined-benefit pension plan, if applicable.

- Delay Social Security benefits.

Source: "Retirement Income: Ensuring Income throughout Retirement Requires Difficult Choices," highlights of GAO-11-400, a report to the Chairman, Special Committee on Aging, U.S. Senate, June 2011; www.gao.gov/assets/320/319396.pdf

---

By reallocating their portfolio into vehicles that better protected their principal—specifically fixed indexed annuities—the couple now can enjoy their retirement, such as it is. Now 81, Jack has returned to work three days a week at the local VA hospital because he enjoys working with patients.

Let's take a closer look at some savvy investments that offer safety for your money and security with your longevity in mind. These can be viable options for your personal, private pension plan.

The Value of Annuities

Equities and fixed income are not enough to fund your retirement. They can't replace the value of an annuity because they don't address the major risk we face of outliving our assets. That's a conclusion of a benchmark study co-sponsored by the Wharton Financial Institutions Center, Wharton School of the University of Pennsylvania, and New York Life Insurance Company (from "Investing Your Lump Sum at Retirement," an essay by David F. Babbel and Craig B. Merrill, fellows at the Wharton Financial Institutions Center, Wharton School of the University of Pennsylvania; http://fic.wharton.upenn.edu/fic/policy%20 page/whartonessay18.pdf).

Government Thumbs Up

Even the U.S. government recognizes the importance—and the necessity today—of alternative retirement investment options with longevity in mind. Its solution: annuities! Annuities are a form of "guaranteed lifetime income, which (transform) savings into guaranteed future income, reducing the risks that retirees will outlive their savings or that their living standards will be eroded by investment losses or inflation," according to the White House Task Force on Middle Class Working Families (www. whitehouse.gov/sites/default/files/Fact_Sheet-Middle_Class_Task_ Force.pdf).

To further encourage the purchase of annuities as part of retirement planning, in February 2012, the Treasury Department proposed changes to defined-contribution plan rules. Those changes would allow people to convert a portion of their 401(k) holdings into an annuity to guarantee an additional income stream in their retirement. The proposal also calls for the relaxing of mandatory required minimum distribution requirements beginning at age 70½ to allow for the practical purchase of what the Treasury calls "longevity" annuities. These are deferred annuities that don't begin payouts until later in life and further guarantee someone won't outlive his or her assets. (www.gpo.gov/fdsys/pkg/FR-2012-02-03/pdf/2012-2340 .pdf; www.treasury.gov/press-center/press-releases/Pages/tg1407.aspx)

There are many variations and combinations of annuities available today. Many of the newer annuity products even offer an inflation protection rider. That's yet another reason it's important to work with your true financial advisor to make sure, first, if an annuity makes sense for your situation. If so, you and your advisor then can find the best annuity product for you.

Guaranteed Income Rider

An annuity product that guarantees your money will last as long as you do is an annuity with a guaranteed income rider that I mentioned earlier. It combines guaranteed growth—ranging from 5 percent to 7 percent annually—during the time period that the owner either pays into or defers withdrawals from the annuity. After that time, the rider then provides a guaranteed income for the rest of the owner's life or the rest of both spouses' lives if the annuity is held jointly by a married couple.

The cost for this guarantee ranges from zero up to 1.25 percent per year depending on the company and product. Normally, the greater the guaranteed interest rate during the accumulation period, the higher the cost of the income rider. The cost is usually deducted annually from the contract value.

Ongoing Income Even If the Account Value Is Zero. There's even an argument that the cost for the rider doesn't matter. For example, an annuity's owners could use their income rider, run the policy out of cash, and continue to take the income. That's a plausible scenario because, remember, the rider specifically calls for a "lifetime" income stream. There's no limitation on how long the benefits will continue.

An income rider also has the potential to leave a death benefit to heirs if any cash remains in the account after the annuity owner/owners die.

The Details. The income rider is a separate account from the actual annuity. Its beginning balance is equal to the first year of the annuity's deposit plus any bonuses the product offers. It then grows at a guaranteed annual interest rate and for the length of time specified in the contract.

When the account owner is ready, he or she can convert the income rider account into a lifetime income stream. At that point, the insurance company will take a snapshot of the income rider account and multiply its value times a percentage to determine the starting annual income amount. That dollar amount then becomes the minimum guaranteed annual amount the owner or joint owners will receive for the rest of their lives.

All this sounds complicated, but it's really not.

Let's look at an example: Todd, 60, deposits $100,000 in an annuity with an income rider that has a guaranteed 6.5 percent compounded interest during its "accumulation" phase. After 10 years, Todd now is 70, and has $187,714 in his income rider account. He then can convert that money into a lifetime income stream. Let's assume the payout percentage is 5.5 percent. Todd then will receive a fixed annual income of $10,324 for the rest of his life.

IRAs and Roth IRAs

The passage of the Tax Reform Act of 1986 and the Employee Retirement Savings Act in 1974 gave Americans a number of different tax-advantaged retirement savings.

Two of the most popular, as I mentioned earlier, are the traditional IRA—anyone can contribute to one, though tax deductibility is limited by income, filing status, and availability of other retirement plans—and the Roth IRA—limited by income, though conversions to Roth IRAs are unlimited. Both, however, offer tax-advantaged growth for your earnings.

Both retirement approaches also have their own pros and cons, checks and balances, and their value to your retirement planning depends on your unique situation. Traditional IRAs, for example, are funded with pre-tax dollars and have mandatory taxed withdrawals beginning at age 70½. That can create negative tax consequences. Roths, on the other hand, are funded with after-tax dollars and have no mandatory withdrawals. They can be a good way to allow your money to grow tax deferred so that ultimately you and your heirs will receive it tax free later.

A COMPARISON: TRADITIONAL VS. ROTH IRA

Traditional IRA:

- Funded with pre-tax dollars.

- Anyone can open an IRA, but tax deductibility is based on income, filing status, and availability of other retirement plans.

- Contributions limited ($5,000 plus $1,000 "catch-up" additional for taxpayers age 50 and up).

- Earnings grow tax deferred (due when you begin withdrawals).

- Penalties for early withdrawal before age 59½.

- Mandatory withdrawals every year beginning at age 70½.

- Prior to age 59 ½ withdrawals may be penalty free for qualified needs:

  - First-time home purchase.

  - Qualified education expenses.

  - Death or disability.

  - Unreimbursed medical expenses.

  - Health insurance if you're unemployed.

Roth IRA:

- Income thresholds to qualify to open Roth IRA ($173,000 to $183,000 married/filing jointly adjusted gross income range; $110,000 to $125,000 single adjusted gross income range).

- Funded with after-tax dollars.

- Withdrawals up to contribution limits are tax free.

- No mandatory withdrawals at any age.

- Penalties for early withdrawals before age 59½.

- Distribution from a Roth is tax free and penalty free if:

  - You've held the Roth for a minimum five years.

  - You're over 59½.

  - In the event of death or disability.

  - For qualified first-time home purchase.

- No income limits on conversions to Roth IRAs.

The Roth Conversion Option

A Roth can be an individual retirement account made up of stocks, bonds, mutual funds, CDs, annuities, and more. Its primary advantages are its tax structure and the flexibility that the tax structure provides.

In some cases, it's possible to convert or roll over other retirement savings vehicles like traditional IRAs and 401(k) plans to a Roth. The advantage of a Roth is that your investment grows tax free. The drawback, however, is that unless it's an in-retirement plan rollover, your rollover is treated as income in the year of the conversion and taxes are due on it.

The question of whether to roll over or convert an existing traditional IRA or 401(k) to a Roth does not have a one-size-fits-all answer. Conversion may make more sense if you're younger and your money has plenty of time to compound and grow. It also depends on your tax bracket. If you're over 70, for example, a rollover may cost more in taxes now than later, when you may be in a lower tax bracket.

In some cases, you can convert small portions of a traditional IRA or 401(k) to a Roth year after year in such a way that your tax bracket doesn't increase, but you still satisfy the income taxes due on a conversion and eventually end up with the Roth advantages.

A Roth conversion may *not* be a good move if:

- You must use part of the IRA money to pay the income tax due. That leaves less money in the account to compound and grow.

- You then may face an early withdrawal penalty for pulling the money out of a traditional IRA before age 59½.

- The added income in a given year could affect your qualification for income tax credits.

- You expect to be in a lower income-tax bracket in retirement than now.

The bottom line is that before making any decision:

- Understand the differences between Roth and traditional IRAs.

- Talk with a qualified CPA before making any conversion.

- Download your free Roth IRA Conversion Guide at my website, www.ChecksandBalances.TV/RothConversionGuide.

Checks and Balances Tools

Download or read our free reports at www.ChecksandBalances.TV:

- The Truth About Retirement
- The Truth About Social Security
- The Truth About Stocks
- The Truth About Wall Street
- The Truth About Income Planning in Retirement
- The Truth About Roth IRA Conversions

For more information on planning options for Social Security benefits, check out the private (non-government) website, PlanMyBenefits.com (www.PlanMyBenefits.com).

Download our free checklists at www.ChecksandBalances.TV to use before buying any major purchase or investment:

- Fixed indexed annuities
- Variable annuities
- Immediate annuities

3 Steps to Financial Success: Know, Check, Act

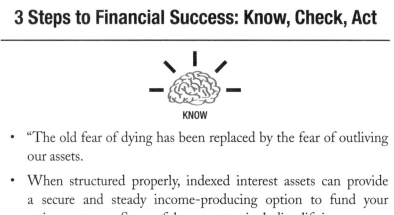

KNOW

- "The old fear of dying has been replaced by the fear of outliving our assets.

- When structured properly, indexed interest assets can provide a secure and steady income-producing option to fund your retirement years. Some of these assets—including life insurance—also can provide a death benefit for your heirs.

- You may want to consider converting existing 401(k) plans and traditional IRAs into Roth IRAs as a tax-advantaged option in retirement.

CHECK

- If you're lucky enough to have a defined-benefit retirement plan with your employer, be sure you choose the spousal-survivor payout option, so your spouse won't be left without anything if you pass away first.

- Compare each annuity company's guaranteed income benefit rider between multiple insurance companies to find the one that will pay you the most in retirement.

ACT

- To be sure the stock market doesn't cut your nest egg in half during a steep bear market, live by "The Investment Rule of 100."

"Everyone hates paying for any type of insurance until they need it!"

— MATT RETTICK

Chapter 12

Insurance to the Rescue
Protect Your Lifestyle, Income, and Assets

We insure our most valuable assets against loss, so why don't we do the same with our financial nest egg in retirement? The New Financial Reality and the insecurities that accompany it demand that we rethink our investment approach. Each of us must be prepared for the unexpected—whatever that is—and be ready to deal with it. Various types of insurance products can not only protect our valuables from catastrophe or loss, but also can provide a guaranteed income we can't outlive.

After all the time I've spent participating in a broad spectrum of financial services—including insurance—I'm unequivocally convinced of the value and security that insurance can provide for you and your loved ones. Yes, insuring all of your valuables will cost money, and no one likes to pay the premiums. But insurance leverages your money like no other investment can. You buy the benefits for pennies on the dollar.

> *What good is it if you earn double-digit returns over time in the stock market and then lose it all because of an illness, accident, or lawsuit?*

Talk to someone who has lost his or her home in a tornado, been in a major auto accident and ended up disabled, placed a loved one in long-term care, or fretted about how to fund their retirement without fear their money will run out. Every one of those people is grateful for the benefits provided them by insurance products.

In early May 2010, an average 15 to 20 inches of rain deluged middle and western Tennessee in a 36-hour period. The Cumberland River through downtown Nashville crested 12 feet above its flood stage.

Thousands of people lost their homes; billions of dollars of property was damaged or destroyed. Barbara Hansen was one of the lucky ones. "We had many blessings," she says, looking back two years after that fateful time. " We only had 8 inches of water in the house. We were the last house on the block to flood, and the first to drain."

Barbara, a now-retired former business associate, also had insurance. Unfortunately, she did not have flood insurance to cover her home (FEMA—the Federal Emergency Management Agency—took care of that). But her auto insurance was a blessing, she says, and quickly paid her what she considered a more than fair price for her flood-totaled 2003 Toyota Celica.

"Both my husband and I thought we would be lucky to get $2,000 for the car. When the [adjuster] said $10,000, I was jumping up and down inside... They paid me $10,000 cash for it, and all I had to do was produce the title. That enabled us to replace that car with a dependable used car and we were able to pay cash for it ...Insurance is like everything else. [No one wants it] until you need it," she adds. "It was definitely worth it!"

It's time everyone stopped bad-mouthing and avoiding insurance and instead thought very seriously about its true value.

The Business of Life

Let's again consider your life as your small business—My Enterprise, Inc.—and you as its CEO. As owner and CEO, you certainly would want to protect your business and its assets from as many unexpected catastrophes as possible. You would want to protect the physical structure and its contents from catastrophes like fire, tornado, or flood. You also would want to protect your business from unforeseen human events—an employee or customer slips and sustains severe injuries, for example, or you are the victim of theft or embezzlement. Various types of insurance policies provide the overall protection your business needs.

Protect Yourself

The same is true for your life. You don't know what the future holds, so you must protect your life and your assets as much as possible. Listed below are some of the financial storms and catastrophes that could befall you—and the type of insurance that can protect you, your assets, and your loved ones:

- You could die tomorrow—life insurance.
- You could become disabled and unable to work—disability insurance.
- Your house could burn down—property insurance.
- You could have a stroke and end up in a nursing home—long-term-care insurance.
- Someone could sue you and destroy all you've worked to build—personal umbrella policy.

I'm not paranoid, and I'm not suggesting that you should be. What I am asking, though, is, What if one of these catastrophes happened to you tomorrow? Could you afford it? What would happen to you? What would happen to your loved ones? These are real questions that have an easy answer—insurance products.

Just as insurance protects My Enterprise, Inc., different insurance products protect you and your loved ones in the event of various disasters and should be an essential part of your financial planning.

169

Inexpensive and Efficient

The most common reasons people give for not having basic insurance are, "It's too expensive" or "It's a waste of money and I'll never use it."

I've been in the insurance industry for more than two decades and I know differently. Insurance policies aren't expensive, and many people do end up needing them. You can't afford *not* to have insurance policies to protect you, your loved ones, and your financial future.

If you're age 45, in generally good health, and a non-smoker, you likely can buy a 20-year $250,000 term life insurance policy for as little as $30 a month. That means for only $30 a month, your heirs can have a guaranteed $250,000 income-tax-free payout in the event of your death.

In the beginning, your War on Debt! and your budget might not leave you much cash after you've filled your various "pockets" of savings. If that's the case, then buy only a small amount of insurance—as long as you have something. Then, as you gain financial ground, increase the values of your insurance policies.

Years ago, even before my family was financially secure, I bought a disability insurance policy, a long-term-care policy, an umbrella policy, and two life insurance policies because I knew what could happen to me and my family without them.

Keep in mind, too, that with life, long-term-care, and disability insurance, the younger you are, the less a policy costs. If you do buy an insurance policy, however, make sure to keep up the premium payments or you could risk losing policy benefits for you or your loved ones.

No Gamble Here

Another reason people often fail to buy insurance is that they mistakenly think it's simply a gamble on their life, and they're convinced none of the "catastrophes" will strike them.

That's a cop-out. Insurance is a simple way to buy protection, and it's certainly not a gamble. Insurance companies are some of the soundest businesses in the world. We hear about the fiascos of mismanagement, like that of international financial conglomerate American International Group (AIG)—which the government had to bail out—but that's not indicative of insurance companies as a whole. I know. I've spent two decades working with and watching the top companies in the business.

Insure Your Life, Valuables, and Financial Future

Insurance products can do much more than reimburse you in the event of fire or theft or death. The right policy (including annuities, which I mentioned previously) can be a safe way to save money and earn above-average interest rates. The right policy also can be a source of ready cash when you need it.

Let's look at the potential of some types of insurance.

Life Insurance—The New Model

I believe that life insurance is the often unsung and overlooked hero in the world of personal finance and investing. The main benefit of life insurance traditionally has been to protect your family financially, providing them with an income-tax-free death benefit when you, the insured, die. But life insurance can have tremendous flexibility as an investment. With the right life insurance, for a reasonable and fair price you can:

- Shelter your money and save on taxes.
- Death benefits are income tax free at payout.
- Save money with above-average returns.
- Grow your money without risk to your principal.
- Fund your retirement.
- Pay for long-term care.
- Provide ready cash as needed (with some limitations).
- Borrow against its cash value.
- Create a steady stream of income as long as you live.
- Create wealth for your heirs after you're gone.

Unfortunately, fewer than half of all Americans who have a financial advisor have discussed life insurance as part of their overall financial plan, according to a recent online survey conducted by Harris Interactive on behalf of wealth management firm, Saybrus Partners, Inc. (see www.saybruspartners.com; www.businesswire.com/news/home/20110816005299/en/Financial-Advisors-Opportunity-Incorporate-Life-Insurance-Planning).

171

The Cost. The cost of life insurance, as mentioned above, is surprisingly low. A $500,000 term life policy for a 45-year-old relatively healthy male costs about $54 a month. If you prefer a whole life policy that accumulates cash value, the cost is about $140 a month for that same male.

How Much Do You Need? In general, an individual should buy enough life insurance to cover a minimum 7 to 10 times his or her annual income. That amount doesn't factor in extra costs for education for the kids, paying off any debts, or burial expenses.

Not for Everyone. Life insurance, like any other investment option, is not for everyone. If you're single, well off financially with no debts, and have no dependents, you probably don't need it. It might, however, make sense to purchase a small term-life policy to cover your funeral and burial costs, or a whole life policy with a long-term-care rider to cover potential long-term-care costs.

Disability Insurance

What happens if you're injured or contract a debilitating disease or in some other way are prevented from working either for an extended period of time or permanently? What will you live on? If others depend on you, what will they live on? How will they make up the lost wages?

These questions can have scary answers unless you prepare ahead of time with the help of disability insurance. Even if you're among the lucky ones who have an employer that offers short-term disability, what happens if you're out of work long term? Without a contingency plan in the form of disability insurance, you—and your loved ones—are out of luck.

The Cost. Disability insurance isn't expensive. A policy that will pay $3,000 a month in the event of a disability costs about $70 a month for a 45-year-old male.

How Much Do You Need? The amount of disability insurance you need depends on your individual circumstances. You must be prepared for the worst. That doesn't mean, however, that you buy the maximum coverage no matter your current income. Instead, look at the various policies and determine the amount of money you will need to make up for your lost income.

If you're looking at a disability policy for a spouse who works part- or full-time and also takes care of dependents, be sure to consider the cost of replacing that dependent care. Too many people overlook that part of the equation and then find themselves coming up short in time of need.

Long-Term-Care Insurance

You need long-term-care insurance. Even if you're comfortable financially, you can't afford not to have it. The cost of long-term care is prohibitive and climbing higher as you read this.

The U.S. Department of Health and Human Service's National Clearinghouse for Long Term Care Information estimates the average annual cost for nursing home care in the United States (in 2010) at nearly **$84,000** (private room). The cost of an in-home health aide is nearly **$44,000** a year, and that's based on a five-day, 40-hour workweek. Assuming the workday is eight hours, what would you do the other 16 hours should you need help? And what about the other two days in the week? An elderly person's needs don't necessarily follow a clock.

What happens if you end up in a nursing home for years? My grandfather Rettich spent 12 long years in a nursing home. He had been relatively comfortable financially in his lifetime, but he wasn't prepared for long-term-care costs and ended up at the mercy of charity.

My mother, on the other hand, was prepared for her long-term-care future. A number of years ago, I persuaded her to buy long-term-care insurance so that four years ago, when she began to need assisted living, she had choices. One day soon she will have to move into a nursing home as her health continues to deteriorate. But because she planned ahead with long-term-care insurance, she has choices. So far her care has cost more than $115,000—and all of it in a large part paid for, thanks to her far-sighted approach to her later years.

How Much Do You Need? The easiest way to avoid the same fate is to purchase a long-term-care policy with inflation protection. The inflation protection is a must because costs are rising so rapidly that sufficient coverage today won't be nearly enough in a few years.

CALCULATE THE COST OF LONG-TERM CARE

The National Clearinghouse for Long Term Care Information from the Department of Health and Human Services has an interactive tool that can help you calculate the cost of different types of long-term care in your area today and well into the future.

Check it out at www.longtermcare.gov/LTC/Main_Site/Tools/ State_Costs.aspx .

Long-term-care insurance doesn't have to be expensive. As with any purchase, though, it pays to shop around for the best policy and price. The least expensive policy isn't always the best value, either.

What to Look For. When shopping for a policy, pay attention to the details. Some things to look for include:

- Will the daily guaranteed benefit cover your needs?

- Does the policy have automatic benefit increases to protect you from inflation. A 5 percent inflationary factor should be adequate.

- Does the policy include coverage for home health care, assisted living, adult day care, and nursing-home care?

- Is the income you receive from the policy not taxable to you?

Long-Term-Care Insurance Alternatives

If you can't afford long-term-care insurance, you do have other choices as seen and discussed below.

One sensible alternative for many people is a modified endowment contract (MEC), which is a life and long-term-care insurance hybrid policy that's overfunded upfront. Any cash-value life insurance policy can be converted into a MEC as a result of how it's funded.

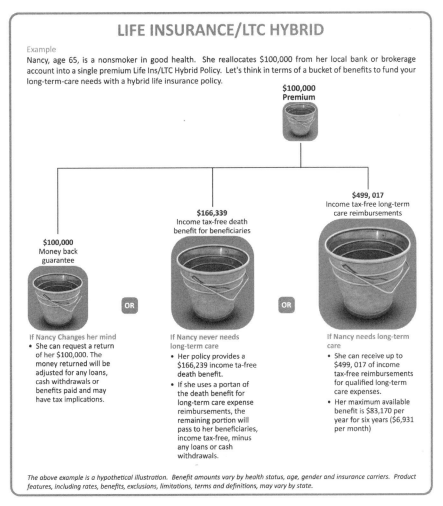

LIFE INSURANCE/LTC HYBRID

Example

Nancy, age 65, is a nonsmoker in good health. She reallocates $100,000 from her local bank or brokerage account into a single premium Life Ins/LTC Hybrid Policy. Let's think in terms of a bucket of benefits to fund your long-term-care needs with a hybrid life insurance policy.

$100,000 Premium

$100,000 Money back guarantee

$166,339 Income tax-free death benefit for beneficiaries

$499, 017 Income tax-free long-term care reimbursements

OR

OR

If Nancy Changes her mind
- She can request a return of her $100,000. The money returned will be adjusted for any loans, cash withdrawals or benefits paid and may have tax implications.

If Nancy never needs long-term care
- Her policy provides a $166,239 income ta-free death benefit.
- If she uses a portan of the death benefit for long-term care expense reimbursements, the remaining portion will pass to her beneficiaries, income tax-free, minus any loans or cash withdrawals.

If Nancy needs long-term care
- She can receive up to $499, 017 of income tax-free reimbursements for qualified long-term care expenses.
- Her maximum available benefit is $83,170 per year for six years ($6,931 per month)

The above example is a hypothetical illustration. Benefit amounts vary by health status, age, gender and insurance carriers. Product features, including rates, benefits, exclusions, limitations, terms and definitions, may vary by state.

A MEC typically has a high cash value that's accessible to pay for a variety of things, including costs associated with a chronic illness and need. Here's how it works:

- You deposit a single premium into the MEC universal product that has life and long-term-care benefits.

- That immediately creates a pool of cash for long-term-care expenses.

- You also immediately have a life insurance benefit that's payable to your beneficiary income tax free.

- There is a guaranteed return of premium protection. If you ever want the money back, it's yours with no fees or penalties.

A MEC can be an excellent option for long-term-care insurance. With the latter you pay premiums every year and never see the money unless you need it for long-term care. With a MEC, distributions are taxed like annuity distributions so you can accumulate money tax deferred and have life insurance protection at the same time.

COMPARING OPTIONS FOR FUNDING YOUR LONG-TERM CARE

Funding Option	Duration of Premiums	Premiums Guaranteed	Deductible Period	Return of Premium	Coverage Period	Inflation Protection	Guaranteed Death Benefit
Long-Term-Care Insurance	Lifetime	No	30,60,90,180 days	If death occurs after 10 years.	2-10 years; lifetime is available on some policies.	5% simple; 3%, 5% compound	No
Life & LTC Hybrid	Single; 3, 5, 7, 10 years payout	Yes	0 days	Yes, after all premiums are paid.	4 to 7 years	3% simple; 3%, 5% compound	Yes; Income tax free
Combination Annuity/LTC	Single	Yes	90 days	Annuity account balance minus surrender charges.	6 years	No	Annuity account balance at death; gain taxable to beneficiary.
Life Insurance with Accelerated DB Rider	1 year to lifetime	Yes	90 days	No	4 to 6 years	No	Yes; Income tax free
Life Insurance Policy Settlement	N/A	N/A	N/A	Client receives a negotiated cash settlement amount based on life expectancy.	Lump-sum payment to client from settlement company.	N/A	Cash payment to client while alive; amount in excess of cost basis taxable as capital gain.

An ordinary **life insurance policy with an accelerated benefit rider** is another option to long-term-care insurance. This is a life insurance policy with living benefits that allows a portion of the benefit to be paid to the policyholder to meet long-term-care expenses.

Some existing life insurance policies allow you to add a long-term-care rider in the form of accelerated death benefits. With the rider, if you need long-term care before you die, you can tap the policy benefit—typically 2 percent to 4 percent of the death benefit paid out per month. That reduces the policy's payout on your death, but it covers your costs and gives you peace of mind.

This can be an easy option if you absolutely don't think you'll ever need long-term care but want to make a contingency plan just in case. It won't pay out as much as long-term-care insurance, but it doesn't cost as much, either, and can help offset long-term-care expenses.

Still another option is a **life settlement,** which involves selling an unwanted or unneeded existing life insurance policy to a third party for more than its surrender value and less than its death benefit. The third party then becomes the new beneficiary and is responsible for all the premium payments going forward. This can be an excellent way of turning an illiquid asset into a liquid one in your lifetime, if necessary.

The money you receive for your policy is tax free up to the amount of the premiums you've paid in. This option has tax and policy restrictions and limitations, so be sure to thoroughly check out the pros and cons.

Umbrella Insurance

Just as an umbrella protects you from getting soaked in a rainstorm, an umbrella insurance policy protects you from taking a financial bath if you're sued as a homeowner, vehicle owner, or other responsible party.

The primary benefits of a policy include:

- **Liability coverage.** Suppose, for example, a contractor you hired to work on your house falls down your stairs and decides to sue you for $500,000. If your homeowner's insurance policy pays up to only $200,000, you would be liable for the other $300,000 should you lose the lawsuit. Do you have $300,000 to spare? Not likely. But, if you have an umbrella policy in place, the $300,000 would be paid by your insurance company.

- **Litigation coverage.** Let's say that when the same contractor sued you, you had to hire expensive lawyers to defend you. An umbrella policy would pick up those fees.

- **Automobile accident liability coverage.** If you're involved in a car accident and sued by the other party, an umbrella policy will provide you financial relief.

How Much Do You Need? Umbrella policies generally can provide $1 million to $5 million and up in liability insurance protection. In today's litigious society, an umbrella policy is a must to protect you, your loved ones, and all you've worked hard for in your life.

One liability claim that's above and beyond the scope of your homeowner's and auto insurance can potentially destroy your financial nest egg. It's not the frequency of claims; it's the severity of a single claim that can wipe out an entire estate.

The Cost. Umbrella policies are relatively inexpensive, too. Depending on your circumstances, the insurance carrier, and other variables, you could pick up a $1 million policy for perhaps less than $150 a year.

How to Find the Right Insurance Company

Identifying the insurer that can best meet your needs is a prime responsibility of your true financial advisor. He or she is the expert who knows where to find the best rates, value, service, and—most important—reliability.

Ratings Agencies

As a Checks and Balances consumer, though, it's up to you to do your homework before signing on the dotted line. You can check the financial soundness of an insurance company through various rating agencies:

- A.M. Best (www.ambest.com): This full-service credit rating organization serving the insurance industry has been around since 1899.

- Moody's Investors Service (www.moodys.com): Moody's is a leading global provider of credit ratings, research, and risk analysis.

- Standard & Poor's Ratings Services (www.standardandpoors.com/ratings/en/us/): Part of the McGraw-Hill Companies, Standard and Poor's provides research, ratings, and market intelligence on companies worldwide.

- Weiss Ratings (www.weissratings.com): Weiss touts itself as more conservative than its competitors in determining the financial strength of insurance companies and banks.

Plenty of Protections

With life and health insurance, insurers by law must set aside legal reserves of more than $1 for every dollar invested with them.

In most states, insurers also must participate in a state guarantee fund pool to protect policyholders (up to stated limits) in case an insurer goes out of business.

> *What good is it to earn double-digit returns over time, and then lose it all because of an illness, accident, or lawsuit? Protect yourself and your loved ones with insurance.*

A Review of the Benefits of Insurance

- Beyond providing financial protection for your loved ones after your death, life insurance has tremendous flexibility as an investment. Among its possibilities:
  - Shelter your money and save on taxes.
  - Death benefits are income-tax free at payout.
  - Save money with above-average returns.
  - Grow your money without risk to your principal.
  - Fund your retirement.
  - Pay for long-term care.
  - Provide ready cash as needed (with some limitations).
  - Create a steady stream of income as long as you live.
- Other essential types of insurance to consider include:
  - Disability. In case you're injured or disabled either short term or long term and can no longer work.
  - Long term care. With the soaring cost of long-term care, including home health care, assisted living, and nursing-home care, you can't afford not to have this type of policy. And make sure it has inflation protection.

- Umbrella. Just as an umbrella protects you from the rain, an umbrella policy is designed to protect you in the event of liability lawsuits. Without that protection, all it takes is one mishap, one auto accident, one misstep, and everything you've worked for in your life can be wiped out.

- Life insurance is a pennies-on-the-dollar approach to financial security for your loved ones after you die.

Checks and Balances Tools

Download or read our free reports at www.ChecksandBalances.TV:

- The Truth About Life Insurance
- The Truth About Long-Term-Care Insurance and Other LTC Options
- The Truth About Insurance Agents

Download oour free checklists at www.ChecksandBalances.TV to use before buying any major purchase or investment:

- Long-Term-Care Insurance
- Disability Insurance
- Life Insurance—Term, Indexed Universal, and Whole Life
- Umbrella Insurance
- Homeowner's Insurance

3 Steps to Financial Success: Know, Check, Act

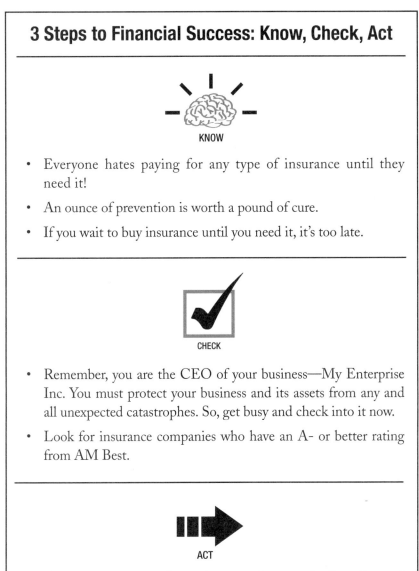

KNOW

- Everyone hates paying for any type of insurance until they need it!
- An ounce of prevention is worth a pound of cure.
- If you wait to buy insurance until you need it, it's too late.

CHECK

- Remember, you are the CEO of your business—My Enterprise Inc. You must protect your business and its assets from any and all unexpected catastrophes. So, get busy and check into it now.
- Look for insurance companies who have an A- or better rating from AM Best.

ACT

- Call your property and casualty agent for an umbrella policy, and your life insurance agent for life, disability, and long-term-care insurance.
- Don't wait until later, because as we all know, later never comes.

PART III
You Can Do It!

"Work with someone who is more interested in your financial security than their own."

— MATT RETTICK

Chapter 13

Don't Go It Alone
Work With a True Financial Advisor

You can't be too careful when it comes to finding the right financial advisor. After all, your financial freedom is at stake. You can't go it alone, either. There's simply too much to learn—and quickly—in order to make the right financial decisions now for your future.

Plenty of people hang up signs, launch websites, and use various media to proclaim their expertise as financial advisors and planners. They work for big firms and small ones; they dress well, exude confidence, and seem to be knowledgeable and trustworthy. But beware.

A big brand name doesn't ensure your money will grow and be secure, either. Financial advisors with well-known brokerage houses as well as those with small investment firms have been found guilty of fraud against the clients they were supposed to serve.

What Is a *True* Financial Advisor?

Anyone can pay a modest fee to have a broker execute a stock trade. But a true financial advisor's suggestions, expertise, and knowledge make all the difference in helping you manage your financial life. A true financial advisor has access to the universe of financial products and makes recommendations based on your unique needs and goals. A true financial advisor advises first.

185

WHO IS A TRUE FINANCIAL ADVISOR?

A true financial advisor has the proper education and licenses to fully serve you; listens to you; offers unbiased and balanced advice; and is motivated by what he or she can do for you rather than by how much money he or she can make having you as a client.

He or she doesn't push proprietary products, has no individual product sales quotas to meet, and so is free to offer clients the entire universe of financial options with virtually no limitations.

A true financial advisor is also an independent advisor who can offer clients comprehensive planning strategies and solutions that integrate insurance, securities, and/or managed money without encountering conflicts of interest from the financial services organizations where the products and/or strategies originate.

A true financial advisor offers consumers the best of all worlds in financial advice and provides comprehensive, all-inclusive solutions that utilize diverse products and strategies to meet the specific needs of the client as opposed to the needs of the advisor or any company's bottom line.

"Put your money in the hands of someone who cares so that you can at least sleep at night, even if everything (from an economic standpoint) is falling apart around you."
—Norma Spear, retiree, Old Hickory, Tennessee, on the importance of finding a true financial advisor

10 Questions to Ask Any Potential Financial Advisors

Don't trust your future to someone simply because they have a sign or website proclaiming them a "Financial Advisor" or "Income Specialist." Before you hand over the keys of your financial vault to a sharp-looking, smooth-talking financial wise guy, interview him or her and ask the important questions.

Don't be fooled by the game some of them play. They ask lots of questions under the guise of learning about your needs and investments.

But they're also sizing you up to see if you have enough money to make it worth their time. Sadly, some might even be assessing your gullibility and whether you're likely to buy into some of their more questionable offerings.

Don't let the agent or advisor take the lead and interview you to decide if he or she wants to bring you on as a new client. Rather, you interview the advisor to determine if he or she is someone you want to hire to watch over your nest egg. As a savvy investor, the real question should be, "Does the financial advisor meet my qualifications? Is he or she—and the company—good enough for me?"

Checks and Balances has a free report and questionnaire online (www.ChecksandBalances.TV) to help you find the true financial advisor for you. Research an advisor first, then ask the questions, weigh the answers, and make your decision. Let's look more closely at the questions and answers.

1. Have You Ever Been Involved in Any Consumer Complaint, Arbitration, or Dispute?

You deserve to know if the advisor you're considering has ever been involved in a customer complaint. If the answer is "yes," that should be a caution flag. You need not immediately dismiss the advisor or conclude that you shouldn't work with him or her. Some frivolous complaints are made by consumers who think they can get a quick payday for some perceived wrong.

However, you should know what happened, what the advisor was accused of, and how the complaint was satisfied. If a monetary settlement was made to the consumer, the advisor may have had some culpability even if he or she did not admit any wrongdoing.

If the advisor answers "no," to this question, dig a little more deeply to be sure. Contact your local Better Business Bureau to find out if he or she is a member and, if so, the "grade" he or she has received. An advisor with any "A" rating or even an "A-" may be fine. Other good sources to check include:

- National Ethics Association (www.ethics.net)
- FINRA—Financial Industry Regulatory Authority (www.FINRA.org)
- NASAA—North American Securities Administrators Association (www.nasaa.org)

- Securities and Exchange Commission (www.SEC.gov)
- Your state's Department of Insurance or Department of Securities (to find your state's organization, www.sec.gov/answers/statereg.htm)

2. What Licenses Do You Hold?

Series 6 ___ Series 7 ___ Series 65/66 ___ Insurance License ___ Other__

The type of license(s) a financial advisor holds determines many things—from how he or she is paid to his or her "bias" toward the products he or she recommends. A license alone shouldn't necessarily determine whether an advisor is good or not so good at his or her job. But it does provide insight into the individual's biases. Let's briefly break down these license types.

Series 6. This is a "limited securities license" that allows an advisor to sell mutual funds and variable annuities. These advisors generally earn their living from the commissions they generate by recommending these two products. Typically—but not always—these commissions come directly out of your investment.

Series 7. This is a full securities license that allows the advisor (a stockbroker) to recommend virtually any security ranging from mutual funds and variable annuities to individual stocks, bonds, real estate investment trusts, options, commodities, and more. Series 7 advisors also primarily earn their income from commissions based on product recommendations. And, as with Series 6 advisors, these commissions typically come directly out of your investment.

Series 65/66. If these advisors don't also hold a Series 6 or 7, they generally do not earn commissions based on their recommendations. Known as "Registered Investment Advisors" (or "Investment Advisory Representatives"), generally they earn fees based on the value of your account every year.

Insurance License. Unless they also hold one of the above licenses, these individuals can recommend insurance products only—like life insurance, fixed annuities, or long-term-care insurance. They earn a commission when you buy a product they recommend. These commissions typically do not come out of your investment but are paid out of the insurance company's pockets.

3. What Standard Must Your Financial Recommendations Meet?
Fiduciary standard___Suitability standard___

Don't be scared off if this sounds complicated. It's not, and it's very important.

If an advisor is held to the **fiduciary standard,** he or she is required to give only the advice he or she would follow in the same circumstances. It is the highest legal standard today. Simply put, the recommendations must be strictly in the customer's best interest!

On the other hand, if the advisor is required to give advice based on the **suitability standard,** he or she can give advice that is arguably suitable. It is a much lower legal standard. In layman's terms, the product you're buying may be suitable but might not be the best option available to you.

These two standards are enforced by different regulatory bodies. The fiduciary standard applies only to investment advisors who hold a Series 65/66, with standards set and regulated by the Securities and Exchange Commission. The suitability standard is enforced either by a state regulator (the Department of Insurance or Securities) or by a securities "self-regulatory" organization like FINRA.

4. What Are Your Professional Designations?
CFP____CLU____ ChFC____CFA____Other____

Getting into the financial services industry is incredibly easy. Anyone who studies for the exam can pass the test and get a license as a stockbroker or insurance agent. So how do you know if the financial advisor you're considering is truly committed to his or her clients and practice for the long run?

A good indication is if the advisor has taken the time to earn one or more professional designations. I don't mean the kind one pays for or that are granted by for-profit companies and earned in perhaps a weekend. The best designations are those from highly credible organizations like The American College and other institutions of higher education. The two designations most identified with comprehensive financial planning are the CFP® (Certified Financial Planner®) and ChFC® (Chartered Financial Consultant®).

A financial advisor who doesn't hold one of these professional designations isn't necessarily incompetent or unprofessional. But if your potential true financial advisor hasn't earned one of these designations, ask why not.

5. How Long Have You Worked in the Financial Industry, and What Did You Do Before?

Anyone can get into the financial services industry, so be forewarned and forearmed! To be fair, everyone has to start somewhere. But do you really want someone to learn with *your* money?

I certainly didn't start out in the financial services industry. I sold everything from Amway products to vacuum sweepers to water filters. But I also have more than two decades of experience, education, and training across many aspects of the financial services industry—from insurance to investing, and from stocks and bonds to financial planning. Make sure your financial advisor has the education and experience to help you make the right decisions.

6. How Many Clients Do You Have?

Depending on a firm's size, there's a practical limit to the number of clients an advisor can serve successfully. Smart advisors have enough staff so they can delegate many of the routine tasks except those that involve meeting with you and making recommendations.

If an advisor has more than 200 clients, he or she needs at least two or three support staff. On the other hand, if the advisor has fewer than 50 clients, you have to ask why. If the advisor recently opened an office and is in the process of building his practice, a small clientele might be fine. If that is the case, however, ask why the advisor opened the new office, how long he or she was in business before starting this practice, and why he or she left the previous position.

7. How Are You Compensated?
Salary only___Fees only___Commissions only___
Fees and commissions___

Financial professionals can be paid in several different ways:

- A salary paid by the company for which the advisor works.

- Fees based on an hourly rate, a flat rate, or a percentage of your assets.

- Commissions paid by a third party based on the products you buy (usually a percentage of the amount you invest in the product).

- A combination of fees and commissions whereby fees are charged for the amount of work done to develop financial planning recommendations and commissions are received from any products sold to you.

> *"The definition of an 'ethical practice' is when your financial advisor is more concerned with your welfare than his or her own."*
> —John Evans, CPA, CFP®, Evans Advisory Services, Erie, Pennsylvania

How an advisor earns his or her income usually drives his or her conscious or subconscious bias. Stockbrokers typically recommend stocks and mutual funds because that's how they earn their money. Insurance brokers push the products they're paid to sell, and so on. A word of warning about fee-only advisors: They're often biased against anything that pays a commission regardless of whether it's a solid investment for you and your needs.

8. Describe Your Typical Client

Pay attention to how an advisor answers this question. You're looking for someone who has experience dealing with issues and situations similar to your own. If, for example, you're about to retire, does he or she work with recent retirees?

Also ask about the average size of his or her clients' accounts. If your account is substantially smaller than the typical account, you may not receive the level of service you would like. If your account is substantially larger than his or her typical account that may mean the advisor fishes in a smaller pond than you're in and may not be able to fully service your unique needs and vice versa.

9. How Often and How Can I Expect to Hear from You?

Weekly___Monthly___Quarterly___Semi-annually___Yearly___
By phone___Email___Newsletter___Personal meetings___

A major complaint among investors is that they don't hear from their advisor often enough, and when they do, it's because the advisor is trying to sell them something. Find out in advance the frequency and kind of communication you can expect, and have the advisor put it in writing.

Top advisors often send monthly newsletters, sometimes weekly emails, and call at least once a quarter or meet with their clients two to four times a year. True advisors call and keep in touch with their clients even more often, regardless of the size of their investment portfolios.

10. Do You Have a Succession Plan in Place?

"What will happen to me if something happens to you?" The last thing you want is to be working with an advisor and be forced to start over again if something unexpected happens to him or her.

Good advisors will have thought through this possibility and will be able to answer your question intelligently. If he or she starts mumbling or seems taken by surprise, you might want to find an advisor who can assure you of future continuity if the unexpected should occur.

Other Considerations in Choosing an Advisor

As a savvy consumer, you should ask friends, family, and acquaintances for referrals when you look for any contractor or service. Find out if anyone you know has had experience with any advisor you're considering. Was the experience positive or negative, and why or why not?

You could ask the advisor for client references, but that can be a waste of time. If someone asked you for references, would you ever give the name of someone unlikely to sing your praises? Probably not!

No matter what anyone claims, all financial advisors are not created equal. Find out the facts first before you plunk down any money or make any commitments. Do your own reality check. Take advantage of reliable sources to find any potential advisor, and then interview the person. It's essential to choose a true financial advisor who has your best interests at heart and not someone who simply peddles or promotes products.

When it comes to choosing your true financial advisor, don't rely solely on:

- Education
- Degrees
- Alphabet designations after his or her name
- Fancy office, appearance, or talk
- Big, well-known company or brokerage firm
- Titles
- How long he or she has been in business
- How many clients he or she has
- The size of his or her staff
- Whether he or she attends your church, synagogue, or mosque.

Although these factors play a role, they don't paint a complete picture of whether someone is a true financial advisor. Other things must be taken into account.

Do look for an advisor who:

- Is more interested in helping you achieve your financial goals than in how much money he or she can make from your investments.
- Is held to a "fiduciary" responsibility, not a "suitability" standard, when selling or offering an investment product.
- Is compensated by fees for investment products and commissions on insurance products.
- Holds licenses in insurance, money management, and securities.
- Owns the same products he or she suggests to you. If it's good enough for you, it should be good enough for him or her.
- Lives by the "Investment Rule of 100" (subtract your current age from 100, and invest up to the remainder, expressed as a percentage,

in higher-risk accounts). You want an advisor who would never over-expose your nest egg to the stock market, especially as you get older.

- Specializes in Social Security benefits and income planning.
- Is well versed on tax-deferred and tax-free investment vehicles.
- Is "independent" and does not work for a bank, brokerage firm, or insurance company.
- Is an expert on IRA distribution planning (Stretch IRA) and Roth IRA conversions.
- Is an individual who you are comfortable with.

Checks and Balances Tools

Download or read our free reports at www.ChecksandBalances.TV:

- The Truth About How to Find a True Financial Advisor
- 10 Questions to Ask Your Financial Advisor Before You Invest a Dime With Them!
- The Truth About Banks
- The 10 Simple Steps to Financial Freedom

3 Steps to Financial Success: Know, Check, Act

KNOW

- Each of us needs a true financial advisor to help us make the right choices. No matter how savvy a consumer you are, there's simply too much you need to know to go it alone.

- Who you hire as your financial advisor is your choice, not his or hers.

- Fancy offices and a listing of professional designations don't necessarily indicate a true financial advisor.

CHECK

- Remember our definition of a true financial advisor—"Someone who is more interested in your financial security than his or her own." You may have to look long and hard to find someone, but when you do it will be well worth it!

ACT

- Be sure to download our free report—"10 Questions to Ask Your Financial Advisor *Before* You Invest a Dime with Them!" You should be interviewing him or her, not the other way around.

"Proper planning prevents poor performance."

— MATT RETTICK

Chapter 14

Covering All the Bases
Legal Documents You Can't Live Without

The proper legal documents *signed* and in their proper place make a huge difference—in your life and the lives of your loved ones. These legal tools can help you maintain control when you no longer are *in* control—whether during your lifetime or after you die, and whether you're a newlywed or a senior nearing the end of your life.

Too often I have heard about an elderly person—or a young victim—kept alive indefinitely on life support. And many of us have seen the chaos that erupts after the death of a friend or loved one as the survivors fight over the assets—big or small. Perhaps even worse is when most of the hard-earned assets of the deceased end up in the hands of Uncle Sam, or are held up for years in probate court.

These and other tragic scenarios can be avoided if only you take the time now to make sure you have certain essential documents in place.

Details Are Essential

Estate planning documents fall into two primary categories:

- Those that will help you during your lifetime.

- Those that will help your heirs, family, and loved ones after your death.

It's absolutely essential that whatever document is involved, it's properly signed by the correct person or persons, as well as witnessed and notarized, if necessary.

Importance of Accessibility

The document must be easily accessible and in its place in the event it's needed. I knew an elderly man in St. Petersburg, Florida, who had completed all the right documents—including a living will and a Do Not Resuscitate order—so he would not be kept alive by machines in the event of respiratory or heart failure. Unfortunately, the 90-year-old had assumed that the safest place for the documents was in his safe deposit box at the bank.

He was home with his wife when he suffered a massive heart attack. Near death, he was rushed by ambulance to the hospital. It was the middle of the night so the bank was closed and his wife didn't have the documents with her. At the time, Florida law required a patient to have the living will and Do Not Resuscitate documents with him or her *on admission* to the hospital in order for the orders to be implemented. The man, in a vegetative state and despite his wife's pleas to honor his wishes, was placed on life support.

The following day when the man's wife brought the signed, notarized documents to the medical staff, the hospital administration refused to honor the man's clearly defined wishes. The institution cited "liability" as the issue.

Sadly—and at a huge expense—this nonagenarian was kept alive by artificial means for several years until his family finally won a court appeal to disconnect the machines and allow their father/grandfather/great-grandfather to die in peace. The man had never regained consciousness.

Find out the best location for your documents; make sure to keep them there, and inform the necessary people about the documents and where they are. If not, you and your loved ones could face needless trauma—medical and emotional.

THE ESSENTIALS

Documents:

- Will

- Revocable Living Trust (it's not for everyone, but can be very helpful)

- Durable Power of Attorney

- General Durable Power of Attorney for Health Care

- Living Will

- Do Not Resuscitate Order (personal preference)

Beneficiary Designations:

- Annuities (with primary and contingent beneficiaries)

- Life Insurance Policies (with primary and contingent beneficiaries)

- Qualified Retirement Accounts, including IRAs, 401(k) plans, and others (with primary and contingent beneficiaries for each)

Online Documents

Although forms are available online for virtually any legal document, I prefer to have an estate planning attorney draw up these important documents, or at least provide me with the blank forms.

People often recognize the importance of various documents, go online to get a blank form, and fill it out, but their wishes ultimately are overruled because they have not used the proper form or not executed the document properly.

If you still prefer to get free or low-cost versions of essential documents online, do so with caution. Such documents might not include the legal language or specific details that apply to your individual situation. Also, certain forms vary from state to state.

Before you download a form, fill it out, and figure you're covered, take the time to research the document and its source. Talk to an attorney who specializes in the particular document to make sure it's properly written and executed or prepared for execution when needed. If not, your wishes could be ignored due to technicalities or simple oversights. This is one area where you do NOT want to pinch pennies.

Let's look more closely at a few important documents each of us needs.

Will

A will is a document that stipulates the detailed distribution of your assets after your death, as well as who will take care of your minor children if his or her other parent is no longer alive.

State Laws. If you haven't taken the time to create and sign a will, your state—like every state in the United States—has a written one for you. Dying without having your own written will is called dying "intestate" or "without a last will and testament." Each state has its own laws (laws of intestacy) that dictate what happens to your possessions and minor children after you die.

If you care about the future of your children and the disposition of your possessions, take the time to have your own will written. A good will should detail who you want to raise your children if both you and your spouse or other parent pass away. Without a written will, your minor children could end up with the sibling you can't stand or with your aging parents or your spouse's parents.

Drawbacks. If you rely on a will to transfer your assets after you die, those assets are subject to "probate." Probate is the legal process whereby your will is "probated" (from the Latin verb "to prove") to make sure it's valid and correct before assets are transferred.

Probate is a public process—anyone who wants to look at your assets can go to the courthouse and do so. That open-to-public scrutiny can be repugnant to many private people.

Another problem with probate is that your assets won't be released to your loved ones and heirs until probate has cleared your estate. Depending on the state where you live, probate could take a year or longer. During that time, your assets are frozen and can't be accessed. If your heirs or loved ones need money in the meantime, they can be out of luck until the probate process is completed or a judge permits the early disbursement of money.

Living Trust

Probate involves the transfer of assets from you or your estate to your loved ones and heirs after you die. But what if that transfer of assets occurred before you died? Your assets would no longer be in your name and therefore not subject to the probate process. Your life and assets remain private and immediately available to your heirs and loved ones.

A retired couple—Eunice and Clyde Sears—came to me more than 15 years ago. Clyde had been diagnosed with terminal cancer and he wanted to make sure Eunice would be financially secure after he died. With the help of an attorney, I suggested they set up a living trust to hold their assets. They set up a revocable living trust with Clyde and Eunice as trustees. After Clyde died in 2000, Eunice became the sole trustee.

I also helped them move some of their liquid assets into long-term secure insurance and annuities that protected them from the roller-coaster stock market losses of the last decade. Today Eunice is secure, just as her husband had wanted. "I have no financial regrets!" she says.

How a Living Trust Works. Your attorney (it's important to have one for this) can help you set up a living trust that holds your assets so you retain full and complete use and control of them while you (and your spouse) are alive.

Think of a living trust as a bucket with a piece of paper taped to the outside. You put things—your assets—into that bucket. On the piece of paper are instructions on what to do with what's in the bucket if you get sick or disabled, if you die, if your spouse dies, or if you both die. Those instructions are legally binding.

A living trust is not an account. It's a receptacle to hold things for you—including accounts—with binding instructions dictating what to do with the assets inside the living trust. You transfer the legal title of your assets into the name of your new living trust.

For example, if I wanted to set up a living trust, I would change the legal title of my savings account from "Matt Rettick" to "The Matt Rettick Living Trust." While I'm alive, as the trustee (in charge of the trust) I can spend, withdraw, use, gift, or do anything I want with the assets I've transferred into my living trust. It's exactly the same as I could do before I transferred assets into the trust with one very important difference.

Because the assets have already been transferred out of my name, they are not subject to probate when I die. They will pass directly and immediately to whomever I instructed, in whatever manner I instructed.

Living Trusts and Estate Planning. A well-written living trust can become one of the most important legal documents you'll ever own and a potential safe haven to reduce or avoid probate and "death taxes" after your death. Federal death taxes (estate taxes) are currently assessed only on estates that exceed $5 million ($10 million if married and your affairs are properly arranged). Note: Any life insurance you own is included in this amount. Although life insurance is income tax free, it is NOT estate tax free.

Children's Trusts and Special Needs Trusts. Other important trusts written while you're alive that can provide huge benefits after your death are children's trusts and special needs trusts. A great example of these trusts is one that's set up to hold and distribute assets for a child, sometimes called a children's trust. If both you and your spouse die, all of your money might flow into your children's trust. You would have appointed someone you trusted as trustee to handle that money. His or her job would be to follow the rules you established about how to distribute the money on behalf of your children in order to care for them.

A special needs trust is set up to receive assets on behalf of a loved one who is disabled and receiving state or federal benefits that would be cut off if the disabled beneficiary suddenly received money. These government benefits are available only to people who typically have no assets; therefore, if you left your estate to this person, he or she would lose the government benefits and be forced to spend down almost all of your estate before again becoming eligible for benefits.

A special needs trust receives the inheritance, and the rules of the trust state that the money in it can be used only for "special" needs of the beneficiary and not for his or her routine care and maintenance. Special needs might mean money for entertainment, travel, and toys as opposed to food, housing, nursing, or medical care. With a trust, the beneficiary doesn't lose government benefits, and your estate is preserved to help provide the extras in life that the government doesn't offer.

Durable Power of Attorney

A durable power of attorney (DPOA) is a document that gives someone—your "attorney-in-fact"—legal permission to act on your financial behalf. A good DPOA can become effective as soon as you sign it or it can spring into action (called "springing powers") only after you are no longer able to make decisions or act for yourself.

Worth the Effort. A good DPOA is inexpensive to set up and can save you unnecessary expense and headaches later on. Let's assume you're married and nearing retirement and a large portion of your savings is in an IRA in your name. The IRA is at your bank where everyone knows you on a first-name basis, so you figure everything is fine.

One day you have an auto accident and are hospitalized in a coma. Your spouse needs money for food, medical bills, and everything else, so he or she calls the bank to withdraw money from the IRA. Because the IRA belongs to you, by law the banker must get your approval for the withdrawal.

Unless your spouse also is an owner on each of your accounts, he or she *won't* be given access to the account in your name. In this situation, your spouse must hire an attorney to file a petition for guardianship of you. Once the guardianship is granted, your spouse must petition the judge to allow a disbursement of your money. In fact, whenever your spouse needs money, he or she will have to file a petition with the judge and wait for a ruling. It could cost thousands of dollars to pay the attorney plus court costs, not to mention the delays and hassle of having to go before the court whenever more cash is needed. What is your spouse supposed to live on and pay bills with in the interim? You get the picture. Get the document, and sleep without worry.

Good and Not So Good DPOAs. Don't rely on an online legal form for this document. A good DPOA is only as good as it is specific. In other words, a document that's more detailed is better. If a DPOA specifically states that the person you're appointing has the right to do something, he or she likely will be legally allowed to do it. If the document doesn't specify that you're giving your attorney-in-fact the right to do something, he or she may not be permitted to do so.

Find a qualified lawyer to write your DPOA. It will be well worth the $200 or so. (Check out the American Academy of Estate Planning Attorneys (at www.aaepa.com.)

General Durable Power of Attorney for Health Care

A living will is NOT enough to ensure that your wishes are carried out. A living will applies to one specific situation—if a person is in a persistent vegetative state and is being kept alive by artificial means. What if you are not in a persistent vegetative state? That's where your general durable health care power of attorney takes over. The individual you designate then has the legal right to speak and act on your behalf.

This document is especially important if you have a significant other and are not married. Without a health care power of attorney, your partner could be barred from any contact with you by a family member and prevented from carrying out any of your spoken wishes.

As with your living will, inform your spouse, loved ones, and medical providers about your health care power of attorney, and give each a notarized copy. If you have homes in more than one state or travel frequently to a certain place, make sure you have a notarized copy with you or with your health care providers in both locations.

Another alternative storage/repository for your documents is an electronic secure online vault. Several companies—including DocuBank (www.docubank.com)—offer this for a fee. You'll get a credit-card-like ID card to carry with you. Place it with your insurance ID card.

Living Will

A living will "speaks" your wishes when you no longer can speak for yourself. Also known as an Advance Medical Directive, this legal document stipulates your wishes regarding artificial life support and nutrition in the event of a catastrophic medical event.

Terry Schiavo and the Right to Die. In recent years, a famous case of what can happen without a living will was that of Terry Schiavo. As a young woman living in Florida, Schiavo suffered cardiac arrest and ended up in a vegetative state due to lack of oxygen in her brain. She did not have a living will, which would have directed that life support systems be shut off.

Instead, her husband and her parents squared off in court for years over whether to keep her alive—her husband insisting she would not have wanted to live in a vegetative state and her parents claiming the opposite. The case, which became a rallying cry for the right-to-die movement, went all the way to the U.S. Supreme Court before her husband finally won out and Schiavo's feeding tube was removed. She finally died March 31, 2005.

Simple and Easy. Most states write and distribute living wills that can be printed out, filled in, signed, and immediately put into effect. As long as it's from a legitimate source, this simple document can be downloaded online and you can rest assured it's valid and legal. To find one, search online for "living will" and the name of your state. Alternatively, you can check for a valid form at your local library, your doctor's office, or a hospital. You also may want to check your state's Department of Health website.

Do make sure, though, that you are getting the living will that's valid in your state. Here in Tennessee, for example, if a living will doesn't include a specific sentence, it's not valid. That sentence: *"I understand the full import of this declaration, and I am emotionally and mentally competent to make this declaration."*

If you have a living will and move to another state, or if you're responsible for helping an out-of-state loved one draw up his or her living will, be sure to execute a living will valid in that particular state.

Make sure the document is signed and notarized. Your doctor and other health providers should have a notarized copy, as should your family and your attorney.

Do Not Resuscitate Order (DNR)

This is a formal, legal directive stipulating that an individual does not want to be revived in the event of a catastrophic medical event such as lung or heart failure. Not everyone needs or wants this document—especially those who are younger or hearty and vibrant.

However, if you have a terminal illness or are in poor health and quickly deteriorating, a DNR may make sense in the event you are hospitalized and facing the specter of your last days in a coma attached to life support. For many people, this document is about death with dignity.

As with a living will, you can obtain an adequate version of a DNR online for free or low cost. They're usually available from your state Department of Health, too.

Beneficiary Designations and Asset Transfers at Death

Make sure the proper heirs are designated on your various assets—bank accounts, money-market accounts, CDs, property deeds, horses, insurance policies, royalties, and more. Even that old life insurance policy from 30 years ago needs to designate an up-to-date heir.

When someone dies or we change jobs or partners, we often overlook changing our designated heir. The end result: The absolutely wrong person—an ex-husband, old girlfriend, or even someone already deceased—legally could end with your assets when you die.

Be sure to properly fill in all primary and contingent beneficiaries on your life insurance policies, IRA plans, 401(k) plans, and annuities. Beyond these designations, you may want to think about a special designation for these assets. Payable on Death (POD) or Transfer on Death (TOD) are excellent approaches for bank and brokerage accounts, CDs, and more. That way, the asset immediately becomes the property of the designated heir when you die.

Checks and Balances Tools

Download or read our free reports at www.ChecksandBalances.TV:

- Estate Planning Documents Every American Shouldn't Live Without

3 Steps to Financial Success: Know, Check, Act

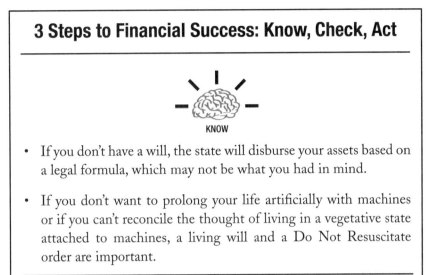

KNOW

- If you don't have a will, the state will disburse your assets based on a legal formula, which may not be what you had in mind.

- If you don't want to prolong your life artificially with machines or if you can't reconcile the thought of living in a vegetative state attached to machines, a living will and a Do Not Resuscitate order are important.

CHECK

- Review all of your beneficiary designations on your 401(k)s, IRAs, life insurance policies, and annuities to be sure they are current and correct.

- Decide who you want to have as your durable power of attorney for financial decisions and general durable power of attorney for health care to make decisions on your behalf, if you're unable.

ACT

- Look into the many benefits of a revocable living trust. Trusts are an excellent way for your voice to be heard—your wishes to be carried out—after you no longer can speak for yourself (as in disability or death).

- Don't procrastinate on taking action with these important documents!

"You have two choices in life: You carry the pain of discipline which weighs ounces, or the pain of regret which weighs tons."

— MATT RETTICK

Chapter 15

Get Started Today
Take Your First Steps Toward Financial Freedom

The first part of any journey is making the decision to take it. Your journey to financial freedom starts the same way. As you've learned in these pages, nothing in your financial life will improve until you decide to make it happen. If it's to be, it's up to you—not your father, not your mother, not your employer, not the government, not your stockbroker, and not your insurance agent. *You* make the decision, and *you* make the difference.

Hopefully, with this book, you've taken the first step. In these pages and online, I have provided you the tools you need to take control of your finances now and lay a course for your future. The next step is up to you. You *can* do this.

A Journey Together

Many others have gone before you and won their War on Debt!—including me. I hope that after reading this book, you too recognize you truly can escape the ever-tightening noose of financial slavery and achieve financial freedom, realize your dreams, and ultimately attain happiness.

As I've said many times, you're not alone in your journey. Checks and Balances (www.ChecksandBalances.TV) literally is at your fingertips. Along with guidance from your true financial advisor, you now have the information sources necessary to chart your journey to financial freedom. Before you set out, though, I'd like to leave you with a few final tips to help you win your financial battle.

Your Financial Action Plan

Now that you've begun your journey to fiscal freedom with the realization that it's time to act, let's review what it will take and lay out your action plan.

Face the Facts

Do a reality check of your life. Look around you and recognize how the New Financial Reality today affects you and your loved ones financially now and into the future. Ask yourself the questions and be honest with your answers.

Is your future secure? Have you planned with longevity in mind so that your money will last as long as you live? What about the financial security of your spouse or significant other? Is that taken care of, or are you at least saving toward that?

Determine what matters most to you in life—your QL. What will it take to bring you true happiness? Take the LifeCheck Quiz in Chapter 4, and pay attention to your answers. They will help you identify your QL. Then, and only then, can you set true long-term goals. Once you know those goals, you then can lay out your plans to achieve them.

Do a reality check of the information sources you've used in the past to make financial and investment decisions. Chances are those sources are biased and may not help you make the right decision for your situation and needs. It's time to wake up, tune out the hype, improve your financial literacy, and learn to make the right financial choices that work for you. Find a true financial advisor to help you. He or she is trained to help guide you on a holistic financial path.

Get Mad!

Start your War on Debt! now. My Enterprise, Inc., after all, is the business of your life, and you are the CEO and CFO. Approach your money with that in mind.

You can't figure out how to achieve your goals unless you know your starting point—where you stand financially today. Go online to Checks and Balances TV (www.ChecksandBalances.TV) to get your War on Debt! and Budget worksheets. Or, if you prefer, make your own. Here's how: Start with two blank sheets of paper and list your income (from all sources) on one sheet and your outflow (debts and fixed expenses) on the other. Subtract the outflow from the income, and the result is where you are now financially. If your outflow exceeds your income, start cutting out and cutting back line by line. Remember, small steps turn into bigger steps, just as small savings here and larger ones there add up.

Start Saving

As you list your fixed expenses, don't forget to pay yourself. It's your future at stake. Put aside money from every paycheck for your retirement. And don't forget your safety nets, including an emergency fund for the unexpected that life is sure to throw your way.

Don't be discouraged by all the different stresses and strains on your limited income. Just remember, you have to start somewhere. There is a light at the end of the tunnel; for some of us, it simply takes awhile to reach it.

Insurance Is Important

Don't overlook the importance of life insurance, long-term-care insurance, and disability insurance. You can't win your personal War on Debt! if something catastrophic happens and you can no longer earn a paycheck. Umbrella liability insurance and health insurance are musts, too.

Invest Like a Pro

When you're tuning out the financial hype and hoopla, make sure the first to go are the get-rich-quick investments. Your financial freedom is about security and steady growth. Remember the "Investment Rule of 100" as you age. Your investment plan must evolve as retirement nears.

Start doing your homework and paying attention to existing investments, including that 401(k) through your employer or SEP-IRA on your own. Are your investments sound and secure? Meet with a true financial advisor and review your current asset allocation. Let him or her help you optimize your growth and security of principal, while lowering your taxes and fees.

Document Duty

No more procrastinating on putting together your will or living trust, general durable powers of attorney for health care, durable power of attorney for financial decisions, and living will.

The Couples' Money Snare

If you're married or in a committed relationship, you absolutely must make sure you and your significant other are together in the battle for your financial freedom. You both must be on the same page, pursuing the same goals with the same approach, to make money matters work in matrimony and outside of it.

Financial Infidelity

One of the biggest reasons for divorces and splits today often concerns finances. Everyone views money differently. That goes for managing it, spending it, saving it, and investing it. We all view debt and investment risk differently, too. That doesn't mean we can't create a working relationship when it comes to money. It simply means it's important to discuss your finances and lay out plans to achieve your goals.

As unromantic as money discussions are, they're essential early in any committed relationship or marriage. Partners—no matter their ages—must discuss money and money habits, and then together lay out goals. Then, with the help of your true financial advisor, you can chart a course to achieve those goals.

The HEART Talk

To help ensure you and your spouse or significant other have a happy financial ever after, have a HEART to HEART talk early on.

H–Hopes and Goals. Start out by discussing your hopes and goals—short term and long term—for the future so you can reach a shared financial vision for your future.

Some topics include:

- When do you want to buy your first home?
- How will we save for your children's education?
- How much should you put away for travel? For retirement?

E–Estate Planning. Whether you're single, widowed, or marrying for the first (second or subsequent) time, it's important to create and update your will, living trust, insurance policies, power of attorney documents, beneficiary designations, and any other financial accounts you both have. If you're not married to your significant other, make sure you have essential documents in place to ensure both partners are taken care of.

A–Allowance Allocation. Together you and your partner need to create a budget that lays out how your money will be allocated. Knowing in advance how much money you each can spend—like an allowance—and how much to apply to your agreed-on expenses cuts down the risk of financial infidelity down the road.

R–Retirement Planning. No matter your age, retirement planning is important, and the earlier and younger you are, the better. Evaluate your current financial situation as well as the age when you and your spouse would like to retire. Then discuss how much of your money should be put away and invested regularly in your retirement accounts.

T–Tax Return. Will you and your spouse file jointly or separately? Are you taking advantage of all the tax credits and deductions available? If it's a second marriage for one or both of you, make sure any tax issues with a previous spouse are resolved before filing a new return with a new spouse.

Final Details

No matter where you are in your battle for financial freedom and achieving your QL—even if you've already attained your goal—pay attention to the details. That kind of diligence will help keep you on the right financial track and stay there.

Shred Old Documents

As part of the journey to financial freedom, each of us must get rid of unnecessary expenses. We must get rid of unnecessary paper and old documents, too. It may not save you money, but it will save you stress-inducing clutter and reduce the possibility of identity theft.

Shred old pay stubs, financial records, and any other outdated documents you no longer need. Save your tax returns, canceled checks, and records that support tax deductions for auditing purposes, but get rid of the rest. If you're not sure whether to keep something, you may want to make a digital record and then toss the paper version. Be sure to shred financial documents and information as opposed to throwing them in the trash. Identity theft is rife in today's down economy, and "dumpster divers"—whether literal or online—can turn a small piece of information into a major headache for you.

Prioritize Your Expenses

When you think you've thoroughly cut everything possible from your monthly expenses, review the expenses one more time. Decide what's really necessary and what isn't. Can you do without that less-than-essential item for a month or two? When you put would-be purchases in that context, you'll be surprised at how much money you can save every month.

Review Your Credit Report

Federal law entitles you to one free credit report from each of the three major credit bureaus every year. Log on to www.annualcreditreport.com for your free reports, and then thoroughly review each of them. It's worth the effort.

If anything on your report worries you or doesn't seem right, contact the company directly to correct any inaccuracies or misinformation. Follow up with the credit-reporting agencies to make sure the error was corrected. It can take a couple of months for the correction to appear on your report.

Negotiate Your Rates

Going forward, every purchase you make needs to include a negotiation. Keep in mind the old saying, "It's not how much you make; it's how much you keep that counts."

Contact your loan provider or credit-card companies and negotiate a lower rate. If they won't budge, talk to their competitors to find a better deal. Remember, these companies need your money. Even if you have blemishes on your past credit, work with the company to get a better deal.

The CBTV Difference

Do look to CBTV to help answer your personal financial questions—in your everyday life and in your quest for your financial freedom. The unbiased guidance and straightforward advice you need to succeed in your financial life is a click away, 24/7. Check us out at www.ChecksandBalances.TV.

3 Steps to Financial Success: Know, Check, Act

KNOW

- You have two choices in life: You can carry the pain of discipline which weighs ounces, or the pain of regret which weighs tons.

- No matter how young or old you are today, there's always time to begin a positive change in your life.

- Remember, you're not alone. CBTV is at your side, helping you all along the way to financial freedom.

CHECK

- Your first step is to discover your QL Factor. Everything else will then fall into place.

- Conduct a review of all of the insurance policies you should have in place.

- Look for a true financial advisor to help you with the right financial decisions.

ACT

- If it's to be, it's up to YOU—not to your father, mother, employer, the stock market, the government, not your stockbroker, insurance agent, or home equity. It's up to you alone.

- Get mad at your debt and pay it off as quickly as possible!

- Invest wisely and confidently.

- Have our HEART to HEART talk with your spouse or with your significant other.

What's on CBTV?

- **Videos:** Don't be misled by other talking heads in the media and listen to a true financial insider instead. CBTV host Matthew J. Rettick introduces a new timely **Financial Headline** each week, **Checks** the facts and **Balances** this information with the real story before offering the **Bottom Line** from his perspective and providing a **Tip, Tool, or Technique** to help viewers make more informed decisions regarding their savings and investments.

- **Financial News:** Get the scoop on breaking news stories in **Financial Headlines** and find out what's hot and what's not in the world of investments with **Today's Numbers**.

- **Financial Tips:** Become a **21ˢᵗ Century Investor** by taking advantage of helpful tips that can enable you to grow, protect, and preserve your nest egg, test your knowledge with **Financial Fact or Fiction,** and learn how to put more "gold" in your golden years with saving strategies in **Debt Free Retirement**.

- **Free Reports:** Help yourself with valuable how-to guides and find out the **"Truth About…"** many important financial topics you always wanted to know more about but were afraid to ask.

- **Free Checklists:** You're never alone when it comes to making major purchases or investments with the help of our downloadable, step-by-step checklists to help you make the right choices.

- **Free Downloads:** If your busy lifestyle prevents you from checking the site on a weekly basis, you can still catch up on archived shows and stay informed with **Audio & Video Podcasts** that can be downloaded anywhere, anytime.

Epilogue: What Life Told Me One Day

One damp gray day in February 1978—long before my financial epiphany—I was driving aimlessly down the road, as traveling salesmen often do. I was desperate to find someone to buy whatever it was I was selling at the time, and I had no idea where I was going—or even what I was doing with my life.

Business was bad, my marriage was rocky (we were arguing about everything), and I had three young kids to support. Exhausted and at wits' end, I pulled into a subdivision under construction and parked the car. I didn't know what else to do, so I just sat there mulling over all my problems. And then I got angry. I actually began yelling at myself, at life, and about all that was wrong in my life, why me, and how I deserved a break.

After awhile I quit shouting—probably because my throat or head hurt from yelling and screaming. Then suddenly I began to write down my thoughts. Those thoughts were what I call "life's answer to my complaints," and they took the form of a poem. The moral of the poem: If it's to be, it's up to me. Even back then, I realized I had to take personal responsibility for my problems.

At that moment, I wasn't ready to take control. But this poem showed me the way out. It took time for me to get there—until that Sunday many years later in a Nashville church. But, as I hope you now realize, at that moment I knew I could get there with the right guidance and help.

I'd like to share my poem and its timeless message with you.

What Life Told Me One Day

I told Life what I wanted one day,

And Life told me, I could start right away.

I said, "I want Riches, Glory and Fame,"

And Life said, "Go get it; you're in the right game."

I relayed, I was tired of living foolish, like a nut.

Life replied, "I have a plan for you, to get out of that rut."

I didn't quite hear the words Life had to say,

But I just knew somehow, I was on my way.

As I planned for the future, and all that it had,

I kept hearing Life whisper, "Get started, my lad."

But as events came up, as they always seem to do,

I left my plans for the morrow, instead of following them through.

Then as days turned to years, I just wondered in awe,

What had happened to Life, and the visions I saw?

The homes and the cars, private schools for the kids.

Not one of them we had seen. Not one we even did.

So I confronted Life boldly, and asked out in a rage,

"What happened to you Life, and the plans we had made?"

What Life then replied with, I shall never forget,

Its wisdom and truth, I'll forever be in debt.

Life said, "I am in you and you are in me,

But you make the decisions, of where you want to be.

I gave you freedom to choose any road.

But you are the vehicle that must move your own load!"

Final Words

Remember, you can achieve almost anything you want in life. But you'll never achieve anything in life unless you take Action!

Glossary

Accelerated death benefit. The ability to tap a portion of a life insurance policy as a living benefit in the event of chronic or terminal disease.

Activities of daily living (ADL). Basic everyday personal tasks like personal hygiene (bathing), mobility (transferring), bathroom duties (toileting and continence), dressing, and eating; ability to perform any or all of these tasks serves as guideline to determine an individual's outside care needs.

Adult day care. Daily care for adults, most often seniors; can include structured activities, meals, transportation, and more; can be private or community based.

Annuitant. The individual who purchases/holds an annuity.

Annuity. A contract, most often with an insurance company, that calls for a lump-sum investment or investments over time for a specific length of time.

Asset allocation. An approach to investing that calls for putting a set amount or percentage of your assets—from cash to IRAs to 401(k) plans and more—into different types of investments with different levels of risk and return.

Assisted living. Accommodations, most often for seniors, that provide help with activities of daily living and include congregate dining, activities, and, in some cases, limited health-care services, usually at additional charge; can be individual apartments or individual rooms.

Capital gains. Profits from the sale of securities and other investments.

Certificate of deposit (CD). Low-risk, FDIC-insured, interest-bearing debt instrument available from banks, credit unions, and savings and loans.

Daily guaranteed benefit. That amount of money guaranteed to be paid by an insurer every day for an individual's care in the event he or she requires short- or long-term care.

Defined-benefit plan. Also known as a traditional pension plan; promises the participant a specified monthly benefit in retirement.

Defined-contribution plan. Includes 401(k) plans; a tax-advantaged individual retirement plan to which an employee and/or employer contribute pre-tax dollars; the employee decides how and to some extent in what the plan is invested; plan value is subject to market performance; taxes due on withdrawal.

Do Not Resuscitate order (DNR). A formal, legal directive that stipulates an individual does not want to be revived in the event of a catastrophic medical event such as lung or heart failure.

Elder law. That part of the legal system that involves issues of importance for the aging and elderly.

Elimination period. In relation to long-term-care insurance, the time period that must elapse before benefits can be accessed; the deduction period.

Equity. Ownership.

Exchange-traded funds (ETFs). Also known as an index fund, made up of stocks in a specific index like the Standard and Poor's 500 or Dow Jones Industrial Average; not actively managed, so lower cost than a mutual fund; not considered a mutual fund because of certain trading specifications and limitations.

Fixed indexed annuity. Formerly known as an equity indexed annuity; a fixed annuity that pegs its earnings on a major market index like the S&P 500 or Dow Jones Industrial Average.

401(k). A defined-contribution retirement plan in which an employee can make pre-tax contributions from his or her paycheck; the employee determines the amount of the contribution and the investment option; in some cases an employer may match a certain percentage of the contribution.

Funeral directive. A formal document (not legal and binding) that lays out an individual's wishes with regard to the details of any ceremonies and burial as well as how his or her body will be handled after death.

Grantor. The individual who establishes and funds a trust.

Immediate annuity. A contract—annuity—most often with an insurance company that calls for a lump-sum investment or investments over time for a specific length of time with payout beginning as soon as it's funded.

Individual retirement account (IRA). A tax-advantaged individual account set up with a financial institution, such as a bank or a mutual fund company; investment grows tax deferred; taxes due on withdrawal.

Inflation protection. For purposes of long-term-care insurance, automatic daily benefit increase to protect policyholder from future increases in cost of care due to rising prices over time.

In-home care. Assistance provided to an individual, often elderly, at his or her place of residence as opposed to that person having to move to an assisted-living facility or nursing home.

Intestate. When an individual dies without a will.

IRA, multigenerational. Also a stretch IRA, an individual retirement account that on its owner's death has no lump-sum income taxes due on earnings; the vast majority of the balance instead continues to grow because only small minimum annual withdrawals are required and thus potentially subject to taxation; also available as an annuity.

Legal guardianship. A formal legal document, or clause as part of a last will and testament, that stipulates who will care for any dependents and how.

Life insurance. A legal contract/policy whereby in exchange for pay-in of a certain amount of money, usually in the form of regular premiums, a sum of money will be paid out to a specified beneficiary/beneficiaries on policyholder's death.

Life settlement. An option for the chronically or terminally ill; involves selling an unwanted or unnecessary life insurance policy back to the insurer or to a third party for more than its surrender value and less than its net death benefit (the amount paid out at death less any debts due on the policy).

Living will. A legal document that stipulates an individual's wishes with regard to various types of artificial life support or nutrition in the event of a catastrophic medical event.

Long-term care. Also known as LTC; the need by many Americans of all ages for prolonged medical and/or physical assistance in a variety of settings; a contract involving long-term care should stipulate the types of long-term care covered or required.

Long-term-care insurance. A type of indemnity coverage that helps an individual defray the high cost of long-term care in a variety of settings in exchange for regular premiums paid; any contract involving long-term-care insurance should stipulate the types of care and settings covered by the policy.

Look-back rule. The legal ability for the government to review a Medicaid applicant's past finances up to a certain number of years to ascertain if the applicant truly qualifies on the basis of financial need and didn't just divest high assets for purposes of free care.

Market capitalization. For investment purposes, can provide insight into the risk level of a company; figured by multiplying the number of outstanding shares of the stock by the stock price.

Medicaid. A state-administered, federally funded government program that provides medical care to the poor.

Medicaid friendly annuity. An annuity that can be annuitized or converted to an income stream for an at-home spouse; must be irrevocable, unassignable, and paid out within the owner's life span.

Medicare. A federal medical program available to those age 65 and up that helps alleviate the high cost of medical care with restrictions and limitations; requires co-payments and deductibles.

Medigap. Private pay insurance, with restrictions, qualifications, and limitations, that is designed to pick up medical costs not paid by Medicare.

Modified endowment contract (MEC). Basically a life insurance policy that's over-funded upfront so it has a high cash value that in turn can be tapped to pay the costs of long-term care in the event of chronic illness and need.

Mutual fund. A company that sells its shares to the public in order to raise money to invest in other types of investments to generate profits for its shareholders.

Net death benefit. With a life insurance policy, the amount paid out at death less any debts due on the policy.

Payable on death (POD). A legal stipulation as part of holding an asset that designates a specific individual or organization receive that asset on the death of the original owner; avoids any delays of probate.

Power of attorney (POA). Naming another individual to handle certain of your affairs when you're no longer able to do so yourself.

- **Durable.** Goes into effect as soon as it's signed and remains in effect should you become incapacitated and until you die or the courts remove the power.

- **Finance.** Individual(s) to take care of your financial matters if you become incapacitated and no longer can do so yourself.

- **Health care.** Individual(s) to make health-care decisions in the event that you're unable to do so yourself; also known as health care proxy.

- **Springing.** Set to go into effect at a later time, usually only when you are declared incompetent or some other event occurs as named in the document.

Pre-existing condition. Medical condition that already existed or was diagnosed prior to an event; with long-term-care insurance, for example, an illness or issue that existed before applying for a policy.

Principal. Original amount invested.

Probate. Legal process in which a will is determined to be legal and valid.

Reverse mortgage. A specialized loan that enables those age 62 and older to tap the equity in their homes to generate income and still live in their homes.

Section 529 plan. Usually referred to as simply a *529 plan;* this is a tax-advantaged savings vehicle for higher education expenses; earnings inside an account grow tax free; distributions are tax free if used for a qualified higher education expense.

Small-cap fund. Jargon for small capitalization fund, which is a pool of stocks in smaller companies—generally those with a market capitalization (number of outstanding shares of the stock multiplied by the stock price) of $500 million or less.

Spend-down. With regard to Medicaid, the necessity of an individual to divest his or her assets in order to qualify for Medicaid.

Trust. A legal entity that holds its assets for the purposes of someone or something else; assets held in a trust avoid delays of probate.

- **Irrevocable.** A trust that's a separate legal entity; directed by a trustee; files its own tax return.

- **Living.** A trust established by an individual while he or she is alive.

- **Revocable.** A trust that remains under its grantor's control and direction; it remains part of the grantor's assets for purposes of taxes; trust assets avoid probate delays on death of grantor.

- **Testamentary.** A trust, set up by a will, that goes into effect on a person's death.

Viatical settlement. A form of life settlement in which a terminally ill person sells his or her life insurance policy in exchange for cash while alive.

Will. A formal legal document that stipulates an individual's desires with regard to disbursement of his or her property and assets after death; can include a *legal guardianship* clause that stipulates who will care for any dependents and how.

About the Author

Matthew J. Rettick, the visionary and host of **Checks and Balances TV**, has committed the greater part of his adult life to educating consumers and financial professionals alike. He is an accomplished author, recognized educator, sought-after speaker, and advocate for personal finance and "longevity planning" for retirement. Matt strongly believes that financial education is the key to empowering consumers, and has educated and mentored thousands of consumers nationwide.

Having personally struggled with debt, and witnessing his family struggle financially after his grandparents faced unexpected illnesses, Matt realized that retirement planning was essential for protecting retirees from enduring unnecessary financial hardship. As a result, he dedicated his career to helping others protect themselves from the depletion of their life savings due to poorly constructed financial plans. Since entering the financial services industry, he has been able to help thousands of retirees create plans that have allowed them to retire, and stay retired, at a reasonable age.

Matt is regularly called upon by industry groups to speak to fellow advisors, as well as by the media to offer his perspective on financial topics to consumers. Referred to as the "Man with the Plan," he has appeared on local and national television, including NBC's *Today, Fox & Friends, Fox Business, Pick of the Week,* and more. Matt co-authored *Fiscal Fitness: 8 Steps to Wealth and Health from America's Leaders of Fitness and Finance* with the late famed fitness guru Jack LaLanne.

The turbulence that the American economy experienced inspired Matt to help consumers recover from the recession through education.

He envisioned a forum where consumers of every age and knowledge base could turn to educate themselves and find their way to financial freedom and retirement success. That vision became **Checks and Balances TV**, an online television show dedicated to helping consumers get balanced financial advice and a platform where consumers can find the truth they need to financially succeed. **Checks and Balances TV** is broadcasted on www.ChecksandBalances.TV.

An avid supporter of charitable foundations, Matt regularly contributes to St. Jude Children's Research Hospital, Habitat for Humanity, On the Go Ministries, and Mercy Ministries of America, among others. Deeply rooted in his work, he is passionate about his calling in life, a fervor that is evident in everything he touches.

Index

Index

Index

Index

Index

Health care power of attorney, 204
Health insurance.
  See also Insurance
    self-employed and, 39
    supplemental to Medicare, 87
HEART to HEART talk, 212–213, 216
High risk investments, 101
Home equity, 7, 34
Housing market, 120

I
Immediate annuities, 125
Income, 68
  guaranteed income stream, 157–158
Indexed annuities, 125
Indexed funds, 128
Indexed interest products, 137–140
  Checks and Balances tools, 146
  fixed indexed annuities, 139, 140–143
  indexed CDs, 139, 145–146, 147
  indexed universal life insurance,
    139, 143–145, 147
  tradeoffs, 138–140
  upside gains, 138
Indexed universal life insurance, 139,
  143–145, 147
  considerations, 144
  policy loans on, 144
  tax issues, 144–145
Individual retirement accounts (IRAs), 98
  beneficiary designations, 199
  financial advisors and, 194
  Roth IRA, 98, 144, 162
  and Roth IRAs compared, 161

traditional, 161–162
Inflation, 99
  annuities and, 159
  bank savings and, 134
  investment review and, 102
Insurance, 167–181
  auto, 168
  benefits of, 179–180
  Checks and Balances tools, 180
  disability, 172–173, 179
  in financial action plan, 211
  flood, 168
  health, 39, 87
  indexed universal life,
    139, 143–145, 147
  life, 171–172, 176, 199 (See also
    Indexed universal life insurance)
  long-term-care, 173–174, 179
  Modified Endowment Contract (MEC),
    174–176
  property, 169
  protecting life and assets, 169–170
  rating agencies, 178, 181
  review, 216
  umbrella, 177–178, 180, 181
Insurance, state department of, 188
Insurance agents,
  commissions and fees, 27
Insurance license, 188–189
Interest rates, on savings, 81
Internal Revenue Service online
  retirement resources, 98
"Investing Your Lump Sum at
  Retirement," 158

Index

Index

Index

Index

W

FREE BONUS VIDEOS
3 FINANCIAL STRATEGIES YOU MUST IMPLEMENT NOW!

I hope this book has been helpful to you and that you now know what you must do to succeed in the New Financial Reality!

FREE BONUS
3 financial strategies you must implement now!

In this video, I will walk you through the 3 critical steps you must take to set you on the right course to succeed in The New Financial Reality.

To get your FREE BONUS VIDEO, go to:
www.AllTheRulesHaveChanged.com/3StrategiesNow

ADDITIONAL BONUS

As a second bonus, I am including my exclusive interview with David M. Walker, former U.S. Comptroller General. David was kind enough to write the foreword to this book. He has a passion for fiscal responsibility and great insight into the financial issues we face as a nation. In this exclusive CBTV interview, David shares his thoughts about what we — as individuals and as a nation — must do to dump debt and build financial strength and security for the future.

To get your FREE ADDITIONAL BONUS VIDEO, go to:
www.AllTheRulesHaveChanged.com/WalkerInterview

The Checks and Balances Financial Success System™ is your map to financial freedom. If you follow it step-by-step, you will become a savvy investor and smarter consumer, and you'll never have to say, "I wish I knew then what I know now" because… **Now You Know!**